Under the
Shadow
of the
Dragon

Under the Shadow of the Dragon

The Growth of God's Church
in Hong Kong

HARRY B. AMBACHER

Association of Baptists for World Evangelism
P.O. Box 8585
Harrisburg, PA 17105-8585
USA
(717) 774-7000
abwe@abwe.org
www.abwe.org

ABWE Canada
980 Adelaide St. South, Suite 34
London, Ontario N6E 1R3
(519) 690-1009
office@abwecanada.org

 PUBLISHING®

UNDER THE SHADOW OF THE DRAGON
The Growth of God's Church in Hong Kong
Copyright © 2003 by ABWE Publishing
Harrisburg, Pennsylvania 17105

Library of Congress Cataloging-in-Publications Data (application pending)

Ambacher, Harry B., 1935–
  Under the Shadow of the Dragon
  Autobiographical, Non-fiction
  ISBN 1-888796-33-2 (Trade Paper)

Printed in the United States of America.

*To the person who modeled Jesus Christ more closely
than anyone I have ever known—my precious wife, Lyn,
who since October 27, 1999, has been like Him,
for she sees Him as He is.*

*And to Teddy and Jennifer Cheng, our beloved coworkers
for twenty years, with our deep thanks to God
for your fellowship in the Gospel from
the first day until now.*

TABLE OF CONTENTS

FOUNDATION YEARS (1807–1969)

YEARS OF PLANTING (1970–1979)

YEARS OF GROWTH (1980–1987)

YEARS OF FRUIT (1988–1994)

TRANSITION YEARS (1995–2001)

FOREWORD

This is a heart-moving saga of God's magnificent exploits through a couple who determined early in their college days to be obedient to God's Word and God's will. When they became aware that God was calling them to the mission field, they humbly submitted themselves. At first they felt God was leading them to East Pakistan (now called Bangladesh), but circumstances developed which divinely directed them to a lifetime of ministry in Hong Kong.

As President of ABWE, I visited Hong Kong many times. I was always impressed with the caliber of servants that God sent to us as they demonstrated utmost commitment and dedication. This was clearly seen by everyone who knew Harry and Lyn Ambacher—they served with all their hearts, souls, minds, and strength. They served with such passion that the Chinese viewed their lives as totally committed to Christ. Several times Harry and Lyn invited me to their home—it was ordinary, limited in space and always located in the midst of the hustle and bustle of that city that never sleeps. Their humble dwelling felt like home as soon as you entered their door, which was always open for anyone who was in need. I vividly recall the glowing, radiant smile on Lyn's countenance as she greeted us and others. She had an unusual way of communicating warmth to everyone. It was like receiving people with her open arms and drawing them close with her heart of love. I further knew that this special place, with its serious limitations of space, was wholeheartedly accepted as home by their three energetic, intelligent, and gifted children. It was within those small rooms that missionaries Harry and Lyn Ambacher sought to rear their children in the fear and admonition of the Lord, and further used their home to counsel, encourage, and disciple the Chinese who responded to their ministry in their church-planting efforts.

I always caught the spirit of enthusiasm when in their presence. You will also catch this spirit as you read the following pages—it is in every chapter. They always started with nothing and believed God for the impossible. Whether they were starting a brand new church, teaching a class in the seminary, administrating as president of the school, or addressing one of the high political officials in Hong Kong, they were stepping out by faith—they were launching out into the deep—they were attributing greatness to God. Their hearts swelled with the conviction that God had called them to be servants to the very needy Chinese people—the largest people group in the world. Their confidence was in the power of God's Word as it impacted a society that was predominantly given over to idol worship.

This is a well-written story. It is worthy of your reading. It will touch your heart. It will make you cry. It will cause you to be thankful. It will give you fresh insight on the price missionaries pay when they surrender all at the altar of God's holy will. It will encourage you through the wonderful ways that God led this couple and their family. It will instruct you in the ways of God regarding evangelism, discipleship, church planting, and the training of national leadership. It will bring spiritual renewal and edification. As you read these pages, it will capture your imagination and make you feel you are working right alongside Dr. and Mrs. Harry Ambacher.

This missionary story deserves to be read by followers of Christ. May God speak to your heart as He spoke to mine in the reading of these pages, and may it result in drawing you closer to the Lord and increasing your missionary vision.

Dr. Wendell W. Kempton
ABWE President, 1971–2001

each week (with a similar amount of time supposedly spent in preparation), I assumed the leadership of Calvary Baptist Church. I also took over five classes that Bill Reid taught each week at a local middle (high) school. Lyn and I both continued to teach at HKBBI. I also served as field council chairman.

Another of the four missionary men, Don Trott, was an enthusiastic young arrival from Hackensack, New Jersey. Don, his wife, Ruth, and their two daughters had just arrived in 1966. Though he had only been in the colony for two years and was still involved in full-time language study, Don was pressed to become the president of HKBBI.

Don Trott was God's provision for us at that difficult time. Don had a tenacious commitment to working with Chinese people and steering them into leadership positions. He began searching for Chinese pastors and church members to join the Bible school committee. The committee worked for months to decide what courses would be best for the students. ABWE missionary Jean Shawver, who arrived on the same ship with the Trotts, taught Christian Education and served as school secretary.

Don was also determined to build a first-class library. He enlisted helpers in the United States who sent current theological books. Putting in many hours at the school, Don was gratified to see HKBBI slowly becoming an educational institution that would attract top-quality students from our churches. The Trotts maintained a busy schedule. Don taught a 7:00 p.m. class at HKBBI and started home at 7:50. Ruth, who was also a teacher, left the house at 7:45 to teach an 8:00 p.m. class.

One weeknight shortly after 8:00 p.m., our phone rang. It was Don. "Harry, get over to my house—quick!"

He hung up. I ran down to the street and leaped into the DKW. I drove the half-mile to the Trotts' ground floor apartment in less than a minute and ran inside. A thin, disoriented teenage boy was sitting on the living room floor, with Don standing over him.

In the fifteen minutes that the children were home alone,

this teenager had broken in and rifled the apartment. Don returned home and was in the bedroom taking off his jacket when the boy jumped him from behind. Don quickly overpowered him and phoned the police.

In a few minutes, police sirens blared outside the apartment. The boy was taken to the Kowloon City police station while Don followed to make his report. He arrived in time to see the police hitting the boy across the face. "He hasn't confessed yet," they said ominously. The boy looked hungry. Don did not want the boy to be beaten, and he decided not to press charges. We never heard of the boy again. Don and Ruth reworked their schedules so that the children would not be left alone again. Thankfully they had slept through the whole incident.

Although more prosperous than the mainland, in the 1960s Hong Kong was a rather poor city, and petty thievery was not uncommon. There was a great divide in the city between the affluent land or business owners, many of them expatriates, and the masses of Chinese factory workers who churned out textiles, cheap toys, and other products. Hong Kong would, during the economic boom in the 1980s, become one of the three great financial cities in the world; yet, even then, wealth would be unequally distributed. Poverty led to petty crime and theft, and later in the century, organized crime intruded. But we never felt insecure in Hong Kong. The police demonstrated a disturbing efficiency, and it was a far safer city than many in America. Don Trott's would-be burglary was a singular occurrence.

While Don headed the institute, I continued to lead Calvary Baptist. The church decided to buy its own property. But this was not the spacious United States, where churches can buy acres of land just for parking lots. This was Hong Kong, with 388,500 people per square mile.[2] The church bought three small apartments side by side on the sixth floor of a twelve-story apartment building a few yards from the busy intersection of Nathan Road and Boundary Street.

My first responsibility in the moving process was to convince lawyers and Hong Kong government officials to process the necessary papers, without paying bribes, so we could move into the newly constructed building. Although the British government was generally cooperative and did not block Christian endeavors as many other countries would have, Hong Kong was plagued by bureaucracy. I rotated among three government offices for almost a year.

When the various permissions were finally granted, Lyn and I spent much of August 1968 overseeing the building project. I supervised the knocking out of the walls between two of the apartments, thus providing an auditorium that seated over 100 people. I left the more difficult questions—should the walls be painted French blue or pale yellow?—to Lyn, who worked with several Chinese women to decorate the new premises.

All the painting and redecorating made it necessary to clean the new auditorium. Lyn was a champion scrubber, and I worked hard to clean the bathrooms. We desired our actions, like the Reids' willingness to invite students into their home, to proclaim our heart for the Chinese people. Even when we didn't realize it, we missionaries were being watched. Several years later, Calvary's members still commented on the missionaries who worked like servants. In July 1968, we were able to have our first service in the building while work was still going on. At the dedication service in September, members were pleased to see how well the building met the church's needs.

Theoretically, I was steering the church and guiding the move to the new premises. Actually, I was learning more from the deacons than I was teaching them. Edmund Kwan, studying at HKBBI, and James Huang, our gifted church pianist, were two of the deacons. They were among the most dedicated Christians that I have seen anywhere in the world. They not only knew more about the church-planting process in Hong Kong than I did, they also had wisdom and experience in knowing how to reach their own people. From them, I learned to see a church as a body of believers functioning together. When I was perplexed at how to find a space large enough to house an auditorium in Hong Kong, where property was unaffordable and even current buildings were too small, it was the deacons who understood how Hong Kong worked, and suggested buying the three neighboring apartments and knocking out the walls.

To be effective in Hong Kong, I had to slowly shed my preconceptions and become intimate with not only the culture of Hong Kong, but the geographical constraints. And most importantly, I had to learn from the relationships I formed with believers. In the same way, Lyn was learning to work effectively with Chinese women and children in Hong Kong. She and Jean Shawver organized a junior church and took turns leading it. Lyn loved teaching Sunday school to teenage girls, and discovered that building relationships with each girl proved the best way to encourage them to study and memorize the Bible.

More and more, our family looked on Hong Kong as home. We began to acquire a mixture of Chinese and British customs. Lyn enjoyed drinking tea. Brent, now two, delighted the Chinese with his "white" hair and Chinese phrases. At age six, Lori, who loved singing through the hymnbook, informed us that she would be "truly, truly angelic" when she played the part of an angel in her school play. On the few evenings we could spare, we attended British concerts of classical music. Lori cried when she learned that in British usage the word lorry means a truck. Seven-year-old Kristi, a passionate reader, read stacks of books with a fine British accent. When Brent lisped his first Christmas carol, we were thrilled to be able to recite the joyful Christmas story together in Cantonese.

The first years of our ministry in Hong Kong had been years of adaptation and building. While we personally built language skills, cultural awareness, and relationships with missionaries and nationals, ABWE was also building: starting the HKBBI, building up Chinese students in preparation for leadership, fostering growth in church congregations, increasing the number of missionaries on the field, and drafting plans for church plants in the satellite cities.

Together with the other ABWE missionaries, we longed for God to bless our efforts and provide real growth in the Chinese churches. But even as we prayed for new life and growth, praising God for His providence in Hong Kong, we were aware of the ever-mounting destruction in the mainland. In the next years, the turmoil in China would have direct consequences for our lives in Hong Kong.

BEIJING, CHINA, AUGUST 1967

"A MILLION RED GUARDS, SOME FROM AS FAR AWAY AS SICHUAN
AND GUANGDONG, CONVERGED ON THE CAPITAL FOR THE FIRST OF
TEN GIGANTIC RALLIES IN TIANANMEN SQUARE. MAO'S APPEARANCE
WAS TIMED TO COINCIDE WITH THE FIRST RAYS OF THE RISING SUN."

Philip Short, Mao: A Life

CHAPTER 8

THE DRAGON THREATENS

When we first arrived in Hong Kong in 1965, capitalism appeared to coexist in apparent peace with communism. In the financial districts, impressive Chinese Communist banks were wedged between lofty skyscrapers. In the bazaars, goods imported from the mainland could be purchased for less than local market prices. The British planted schools throughout Hong Kong, seeing education as a tool to shape the colony, but at least forty Communist schools also existed in Hong Kong, with an enrollment of over 20,000 students. Communism was a silent influence under the surface of life in Hong Kong.

On special holidays, particularly October 1, the Communist national holiday commemorating Mao's takeover of China on October 1, 1949, banks and stores were decorated with huge portraits of Chairman Mao. Many Chinese had moved to the colony in search of freedom, but they loved their home country. In their flight from Communist oppression, they had left behind entire lives, and people from Hong Kong traveled daily by train to China, some on business, many visiting relatives or friends. Even during Mao Tse-tung's rise to power, the border between the colony and the mainland was still somewhat permeable. The economic relationship between Hong Kong and China was one of mutual gain: Hong Kong was dependent on China for the supplies of food and water entering the colony daily by junk, truck, and train. China, in turn, derived revenues and an inflow of cash from the colony—as Chairman Mao had admitted, "Hong Kong is useful to us."

But by late 1950, almost all foreigners had fled China, and the exodus of Chinese refugees had begun in earnest. Inhabitants of Hong Kong often repeated the proverb, "When China sneezes, Hong Kong gets a cold." Since 1841, Hong Kong's geographical proximity to and economic dependence on the mainland had made it vulnerable to events just across the border in China. As Mao Tse-tsung's red Communist sun rose higher on the mainland, a chill crept over the colony. The previously harmless signs of Communist influence—the banks, the propaganda schools, the posters of Mao on holidays—began to cause more anxiety.

Throughout the 1960s, conditions on the mainland deteriorated drastically. Chairman Mao proclaimed that he would harness the power of the masses and transform China into an industrial power in one "Great Leap Forward." Instead, his plan resulted in mass starvation. In *Mao: A Life,* Philip Short writes: "In 1959 and 1960, some twenty million Chinese starved to death. Five million more perished from hunger in 1961."[1]

Mao blamed the famine on ideological failure of many of the leaders and people. In 1966, he launched "The Great Proletarian Cultural Revolution." The leaders of the Cultural Revolution sought to destroy the four traditional elements of Chinese society: old customs, habits, culture, and thinking.[2] Only revolution could purge the masses of their alleged corruption; only revolution could silence Mao's opponents. Under Mao's encouragement, a million Red Guards from all over the country converged on Beijing. Within days, they attacked leaders, teachers, parents, and authority figures.

All schools and colleges were closed. Books were burned in mass bonfires, while the "Little Red Book" of Mao's sayings was exalted to biblical status. Communism was the one and only ideology; all others were proclaimed false. Those who dared to oppose Communist doctrine were killed. The Red Guards shaved the heads of their victims, made them kneel, and beat them. Thousands of intellectuals were beaten to death. Under the red sun, the mainland ran with blood.

By 1967, China's government had practically ceased to function. Far from purging ideological conflict and uniting the proletariat, the bloody revolution only escalated factional violence. Philip Short reports: "At Chongqing, in southern China, rival groups used anti-aircraft guns to bombard each other's positions. In nearby Changsha, they used missiles."[3]

In Hong Kong, we watched with horror; yet though we spoke with Chinese refugees, we could barely begin to fathom the terror they had experienced. Lyn's Cantonese teacher, Ann Luciano, began to weep one day as she discussed the growing persecution in China. "Oh, Lyn, Lyn," she cried, "Americans cannot know. They cannot care. They are too far away, and they have never suffered." Ann had spent several months in a Communist prison, enduring humiliation and witnessing unspeakable atrocities. She had seen the suffering of her country, its cities and its people. Though she had been able to flee to Hong Kong, where she became a member of Calvary Baptist Church, her family still lived in China.

We met members of our churches who had escaped from China. Chu Ming-kwong had crept across the border to the New Territories through a deep fog. Chan Ping-fai had swum more than ten miles to freedom, falling exhausted on a beach. The Communist government banned basketball in the provinces of Southern China that were adjacent to Hong Kong, because so many people were trying to use basketballs as flotation devices to help swim across the border.

For Americans across the Pacific Ocean, the Cultural Revolution may have seemed abstract and distant; but in Hong Kong the effects became more and more tangible, as the corpses of the Chinese dead began to wash up on our shores.[4] It was inevitable that the violence would spread across the border into Hong Kong. On May 6, 1967, a group of workers who had been fired by the Hong Kong Artificial Flower Works picketed in front of the factory. When the workers tried to prevent trucks from leaving the factory, twenty-one men were arrested for physically resisting the police. The British government reported the conflict as a minor incident, with little or no violence, and no serious injuries incurred.[5]

The Hong Kong Communists, however, seized on the incident as an opportunity to stage demonstrations against the British government. In Hong Kong, there was already economic inequity between the working-class factory workers and the upper-class factory owners. Headlines appeared in Communist newspapers throughout Hong Kong, denouncing the government and accusing the police of attacking unarmed workers. The workers' union demanded the workers be released from prison and paid compensation by the government. Meetings were held, and posters began to appear around the city, attacking the government and protesting police brutality. Demonstrations continued at the factory, attracting larger and larger crowds.

When the picketers threatened to break into the factory on May 11, a further clash with the police erupted. This time, serious rioting broke out, which spread from the streets near the factory to adjacent areas of Kowloon. For three days mobs battled the police, setting fire to buses and other vehicles, and looting government offices. Students in Kwun Tong told us that they had been paid $1 each by older men to throw stones at the police. For the first time since World War II, a curfew was imposed in Kowloon. From the roof of our apartment building, we watched the streets fill with the smoke and flames of burning buses, as police sirens shattered the night. It took three days before the British restored calm.

Undeterred by the calm, the Communists stepped up their campaign and formed an "All-Circles Anti-Persecution Struggle Committee," with membership drawn from all Communist organizations in the colony. Spurred on by Communist newspapers, delegations began to converge on Government House with petitions. Powerful loudspeakers were mounted on the Bank of China building in the central business district of Hong Kong Island, blaring out propaganda. The Communists accused the British government of employing imperial force to persecute the Chinese workers and suppress their rebellion. The British, in their words, were invading colonizers, exploiting Hong Kong for capitalist gain.

A week later, the British government announced that individual petitions to the governor would be permitted, but delegations would be limited to twenty people. More than 1,000 people challenged this order, and the following morning, an angry crowd of protestors formed in front of the Hilton Hotel, only a few blocks from Government House. Fighting broke out, and for the first time in the colony's history, a curfew was also imposed on Hong Kong Island.

We were not sure what the Communists' real goals were, but suddenly, missionaries were conscious of being foreigners in Hong Kong. Our movements became limited, for the curfews imposed to preserve order also prevented us from going to language school. We sensed a change in the way many Chinese people looked at British and Americans, as if we too were invaders, oppressors. When we went out in public, tension rippled almost visibly.

One oppressively hot afternoon, Lyn took the children to swim at a public park less than a mile from our apartment. In

Freedom Now, a Christian magazine, she described her initial unease entering the pool:

> As I pushed the baby's stroller up the long hill the last block to the swimming pool, the two girls chattering happily beside me, I felt vaguely uneasy, as usual. Yet, our neighborhood and our pool were integrated. We paid our taxes; we bought our pool tickets. We had every right to be here, I reminded myself. And besides, the day was so hot; the children loved the water so much.
>
> When we entered the pool, there was a change in the atmosphere. Strange, I mused, we were as clean, as well-dressed, as well-behaved as anyone there. It was because of our color, only our color . . . A few little boys began teasing my girls, then splashing them unmercifully. I said a few quiet words to them but saw that it was useless. So I spoke to the girls: "Come on, we'll go to the wading pool." The joy went out of their faces, but they followed me obediently to the "baby" pool.

When Lyn and the children arrived at the baby pool, they were followed by the other children. First forty, then fifty, then 100 youths left the adult pool to surround Lyn and the girls at the wading pool: "The teasing changed to taunting and angry shouts: *'Gwailo, gwailo!'* Soon they were not just splashing, but throwing water at us. When I looked at the guards for help, I discovered both had turned their backs and were staring intently in another direction."

Shielding the baby and the whimpering girls, Lyn fled with them toward the dressing room, fearing a further explosion of hostility. Afterwards, the girls asked, "Why, Mommy, why? Why can't we swim, too?" Lyn responded, "Because you're white, darling, because you're white." This experience brought home the ugliness of racism to us. For the first time, we felt the animosity behind *gwailo,* the Cantonese word for "foreign devil."

As the political climate grew more hostile toward foreigners, the American Consulate warned me, as the field council chairman, that all our missionaries needed to be ready to evacuate within twenty-four hours. The contingency plan was that each person could take one suitcase, and we would be flown initially to Manila. In response, a group of missionaries gathered in our home for prayer. Our prayers were simple and direct. We believed God had brought us to Hong Kong. He could keep us there if He chose to do so. We asked Him to allow us to remain, if it was His will. Several other missions had already evacuated their people.

We prayed for His protection of our families and for His peace on the city. We did not want to leave and abandon the Chinese Christians. We were aware that we were seeing history made before our eyes. If anything, we hoped that the turmoil fostered by the Communist propaganda would open more doors to the Gospel, as people recognized the ugly reality behind the Communist doctrine and yearned for true peace. One day went by, then another, and still the Consulate did not give the order to evacuate. Slowly, one day at a time, the crisis seemed to ease.

Increasingly, it became evident the Hong Kong Communists were not supported by a large percentage of Hong Kong's population. The Communists called for a general strike of all Chinese workers on June 24, 1967, but it was not a success, and the factories kept rolling. Life struggled on in the tense environment of Kowloon; we kept attending language classes when curfews permitted, buying at the markets as we needed. While we observed caution in all our activities, incidents like Lyn's encounter at the pool were rare.

Still, though the majority of the population was not interested in revolution, the hostilities continued to erupt at intervals. In late June, at a town in the New Territories on the border with China, 200 people attacked a police post. On July 8, Kowloon seemed to be quieting down, and we dared to go to Jimmy's Kitchen, a restaurant on Hong Kong Island, to celebrate Lyn's birthday.

When we came out of the restaurant, we heard the sounds of a riot in the distance. In the New Territories, people had attacked another police post, and the police had opened fire with wooden projectiles. The people responded with machine gun fire, and five policemen were killed. Now the violence was erupting on Hong Kong Island. The bellows of angry voices and the crash of bodies rushed towards us, and we realized the crowd was moving closer. Walking with great haste, we moved east as quickly as we could with the three children and made our way to the Star Ferry. Once on the ferry, we rode six minutes across the harbor to Kowloon and were soon out of danger, but we wondered how much longer the trouble would continue.

On July 12, British police began a series of raids on Communist buildings, seizing weapons and explosives, and making arrests. In August, Communists responded by attacking a popular radio announcer, Mr. Lam Bun, who had strongly criticized the Communists. They drenched him and his cousin in gasoline and burned them to death. The Communists also planted bombs throughout the colony on an almost daily basis until the end of December. Altogether, fifty-one people were killed. The horrific bombings and burnings revealed the Communists as the true persecutors and turned the population strongly against them. As the police were able to shut down the terrorist networks, the riots and conflicts began to subside. Through it all, God protected the missionaries, and enabled us to stay and work in Hong Kong.

But even as the riots and attacks began to subside, we were hit by another crisis with more effect on our daily lives. Hong Kong had always been dependent on the mainland for its water supply, for the rainfall on its small land area was not sufficient for the huge population there.[6] For over 100 years, the system of reservoirs had been expanded continually, yet water still had to be imported from China. From August 1966 to June 1967, Hong Kong experienced its driest period on record.[7] In 1967, Hong

Kong was hit by the worst water shortage in its history, at the same time that China collapsed into revolution and anarchy.

Water levels in reservoirs dwindled day by day. Although the Chinese had contracted to sell water to Hong Kong during the summer months, after the riots started, "It proved impossible to make contact with the Chinese authorities," according to the government yearbook.[8] Hong Kong's dependence on China for water was suddenly revealed as a dangerous vulnerability. Water restrictions began in February, when the supply was reduced to sixteen hours a day. In June it was cut again, to eight hours a day. By July it was necessary to reduce the supply to four hours every other day, and then to a mere four hours every fourth day.

We had taken the availability of water for granted, never thinking about it until it was gone. When the supply became available for only a few hours every fourth day, our family's entire life seemed to revolve around water. Thirst and grime settled on us until all we could think of was being clean. We waited and planned anxiously for our neighborhood's turn for water. The pipes in our building were turned on at four in the afternoon. Rushing frantically, we washed dishes and started the washing machine. Everyone took a bath as quickly as possible. I filled buckets in a back room, while Lyn collected water for dishes for the next three days. The water was turned off again promptly at eight in the evening.

With Brent still in cloth diapers (before the days of disposables), we found the water shortage a taxing business; but our hardships were insignificant compared to those our Chinese friends suffered. One Friday evening, our Cantonese tutor, Mr. Ho, came to teach our character-writing class. He was almost in tears, and we quickly asked why. He lived near the top of a twenty-story apartment building. When it came time to receive their water on the fourth day, everyone in the building turned on the taps at once. The pressure in the pipes was simply not strong enough, and people on the top floors of the building got no water at all. Mr. Ho and his wife had to wait for an emergency water truck to come to their neighborhood. They were only able to fill several buckets to carry back to their apartment.

Enough rain finally fell to end the water shortage in October 1967. Hong Kong had survived the dragon's threat. But the physical thirst of Mr. Ho and his wife reminded us of the spiritual thirst of the Chinese people. God had protected the ABWE missionaries for a purpose—that they might share Christ, the Living Water, with the people of Hong Kong.

Not long after we had been spared from the threats of riots and water shortage, another event made me personally aware of God's protection in my life. On the Saturday before Christmas 1968, I made my way home after a typically bruising touch-football game. It was cold, and as I entered the small bathroom to take a shower, I turned on our kerosene heater. Unaware that it wasn't working properly, I luxuriated in the hot water while the heater burned up all the oxygen in the air. When I started to get out of the shower, the room began to spin. The last thought I had was that somehow I should get the bathroom door open. As I fell to the floor, I managed to hit the doorknob and crack the door just a few inches. Those few inches saved my life.

Lyn found me on the floor a few minutes later, unable to walk or talk. The doctor said I had been just a few minutes away from a permanent furlough. Bill Commons came to the house, and with tears streaming down his cheeks, told me that he had been praying for me. I lay in bed and pondered deeply. I was grateful to God for sparing me. After a few hours in bed with blankets piled on me, I was able to move again.

The very next day, on Sunday afternoon, ABWE church-planter Merle Buckingham and Missionary Aviation pilot George Raney were killed in a plane crash in the Southern Philippines. I was not in the habit of asking why God did what He did. But now I certainly did wonder. There had been two accidents twenty-four hours and five hundred miles apart. Merle had been taken to heaven; I had been left in Hong Kong.

It was one of the most sobering events in my life. I wasn't sure why God had chosen to spare me, a young, inexperienced missionary, rather than Merle, a veteran. How could I know His whole purpose for my life? But after I returned from furlough, I was determined to use the time He had given me to accomplish His work in Hong Kong: planting churches and building up HKBBI.

Harry and Teddy at one of the Wo Lok baptisms in the 1980s

Wo Lok Estate in Kwun Tong

中國浸信會神學院
CHINA BAPTIST THEOLOGICAL COLLEGE
三樓 FLAT A 2 F

China Baptist
Theological College's
newly purchased
quarters, 1980

Lyn's Sunday school
class at Wo Lok Baptist
Church, 1980s

WO LOK BAPTIST CENTER
和樂浸信會閱覽中心

Teddy Cheng and Norm Barnard in
front of Wo Lok Baptist Church, 1981

Shun On Estate, 1983

Gloria and Bill Reid
at CBTC, 1983

Some members at Shun On

1970–1979

YEARS OF PLANTING

HONG KONG ISLAND, 1970

"HONG KONG EMERGES THIS YEAR FROM THE DECADE OF THE SIXTIES
AS IT ENTERED, SURGING FORWARD AT AN INCREASING PACE.
IT HAS RISEN TO A PLACE AMONG THE 25 LEADING TRADING COUNTRIES
IN THE WORLD."

Hong Kong Government Press

CHAPTER 9

MOVING TO A SATELLITE CITY

In May 1969, after our first four years on the field, we returned to Ohio on furlough. For the next thirty years, we would alternate four years on the field with one year of furlough. In 1969, we had just completed four years of language study, and found it difficult to pack up and go "home" just when we were finally becoming proficient in Cantonese and acclimated to the culture. Lyn was probably happiest to return to the United States—so much space, so much grass, so much sky—and be reunited with her loved ones. For our children, furlough was both exciting and confusing—to them, home was Hong Kong, not Ohio. They were suddenly plunged into a different culture and a whole new network of family and relatives. Nor was furlough a period of rest after the exertions of the field; instead, I embarked on a whirlwind tour of churches, reporting God's work in Hong Kong to our supporters.

During our absence from Hong Kong, Don Trott continued as the second president of the Bible institute. On June 9, 1969, HKBBI had its first graduation, as Tommy Tang and Yeung Po-wan finished the three-year course. Our vision of finding Chinese pastors to lead the Hong Kong churches was finally being realized: Tommy Tang was asked to return to Calvary Baptist Church as an associate pastor, and Yeung Po-wan continued as pastor of Sunshine Baptist. That summer, Po-wan married fellow HKBBI student Miranda Wan. Lyn and I rejoiced to hear of these first fruits of the Bible institute's leadership training. In the next decades, under the leadership of Chinese nationals trained at HKBBI, the ABWE churches would grow substantially.

We rented a house with an acre of land outside our hometown of Ashland, Ohio. We thrilled again at the beauty of the turning of the leaves. When winter came, Brent was so excited by the first snowfall of his life that he refused to put on gloves and soon came inside crying with his hands stinging from the cold.

In the midst of the happy preparations for Christmas, the news of Joan Reid's sudden death in Hong Kong on December 17, 1969, shattered our joy. The Reids had returned to Hong Kong in July and were just making the first contacts towards planting their second church, Faith Baptist, when Joan died unexpectedly. Our hearts ached as we prayed for Bill and his family. The Reids had been the couple to whom we were closest in Hong Kong. I had never thought I could start a church—but watching Bill, learning from him, I had begun to think, "Yes, I can." Now, once again, the sudden death of a missionary tore a hole in our hearts and plans.

The field council asked us to choose between two possible assignments for the coming four-year term: returning to the Bible institute full time or starting a church. It was now two years since the field council had indicated the urgent need for church plants in the new satellite cities, yet Kwun Tong still stood empty. At the school, full-time teachers and leaders were badly needed, especially without the Reids. We knew HKBBI was essential for the future of our entire work in Hong Kong, but we were also aware of the tremendous need in the satellite cities. We finally asked the field council for the assignment of starting a new church in Kwun Tong.

This first satellite city, six miles east of Kowloon, had been a landfill until the British government began development there in 1955. By 1970, 641 acres of new land had been formed, mostly by reclamation from the sea. More than 500 factories now operated there, employing 12 percent of Hong Kong's industrial work force. Over 160,000 people already lived in Kwun Tong.[1] In the 1970s, the strife caused by the Communist riots had been replaced by slowly increased affluence, and Hong Kong was poised for yet more population growth.

During the last few months of our furlough ministry, we traveled among supporting churches, reporting what God had done during our first term and speaking of the challenge ahead in the satellite cities. Letters from friends in Hong Kong warned us that the colony was in the midst of the worst housing shortage in its history. Some businessmen had been living with their families in hotels for as long as six months because no apartments were available. Hong Kong's history already seemed like one long, continuous housing shortage to us. If this were worse, it must be unimaginable. We urged friends in every church to pray specifically that God would open up the exact apartment He knew would be best for us.

* * *

We returned to Hong Kong late on August 10, 1970, this time by plane—no more turbulent sea passages for Lyn. As we flew through the Lei Yue Mun Pass, we were fascinated again by the spectacle of lights. White, orange, green, and red, the signs and lights and lamps flashed out from every inch of the city, transforming the night into a bright blur of color. We rested in a hotel trying to shake off jet lag, but woke up at four in the morning and walked to an all-night coffee shop for breakfast. Meandering down dirty streets through the hot, humid night, Lyn and I wondered why we had come back to this urban jungle. The air was thick with pollution; the city was a cauldron of sweat and noise and restless energy. But four-year-old Brent danced on the street and called out, "Isn't it just *great* to be back in Hong Kong?"

So we began our search for an apartment, journeying to Kwun Tong to survey the possibilities. We did not want to live in a large, expensive apartment that might cut us off from average Chinese people, so we prayed for a small, but adequate place right in the middle of Kwun Tong. Bob Paswaters, who had been one of the missionaries to meet us at the dock when we arrived in 1965, reminded us of the housing shortage and tactfully warned me not to be too disappointed if nothing turned up right away.

We paced along Yuet Wah Street, asking the watchmen sitting at the front gate of each apartment building if there were any flats to rent. Government resettlement estates provided most of the housing in Kwun Tong, for which we, as foreigners, were not eligible. Only these privately owned buildings on Yuet Wah Street rented flats. We turned up just one lead—an apartment of 600 square feet in a good location. It included a living room, three bedrooms, and a kitchen. But the watchman insisted it was not for rent, only for sale. We asked to see the owner.

The landlord, Mr. Chan, agreed to meet us at the apartment. Since he spoke Mandarin rather than Cantonese, we took a friend who spoke both dialects to interpret for us.

"Mr. Chan," I explained, "we are missionaries, and our mission policy does not permit us to buy an apartment.[2] But we have come to Kwun Tong to meet people and tell them about Jesus Christ. We plan to stay for four years, and I would like to rent your apartment."

As he listened to the translation, Mr. Chan broke into a big smile. "I am also a Christian," he exclaimed. "I retired and came down from northern China to be near family. I had hoped to start a church here in Kwun Tong, but since I can't speak Cantonese, I found that to be impossible. I will gladly rent the flat to you. Stay as long as you like. All I ask is that you phone me the night before you leave and bring me the key."

As Lyn and I looked at each other in joy, Mr. Chan stuck out his hand. "Give me your hand," he said, shaking my hand vigorously. "Christians don't need pieces of paper for contracts. This is the only lease we need."

He was as good as his word, and we never had a better landlord on either side of the world. Whenever we met Mr. Chan on the street, although we could not understand all of his Mandarin, we knew he was asking about the progress of the church. We were amazed to see how God had both answered our need for an apartment and fulfilled Mr. Chan's desire to see churches planted in Kwun Tong—once again, He was directing every step of our lives.

We rented a truck and moved our furniture to the new flat. Stacking it around the apartment as best we could, we found sheets to make the beds and fell asleep. The next morning was one of the most overwhelming times of our lives. We woke up to a city of several hundred thousand people where we didn't know a single person, except for Mr. Chan—and we couldn't even talk to him.

Where were we to start? We knew people in Hong Kong did not generally welcome door-to-door visitation. The Cantonese people, while open to friendly conversation, were much like Americans or Londoners in big cities: rushing from business to home, valuing their privacy, and struggling to preserve their personal space in the cramped housing settlements. We prayed that God would clearly give us a way to meet people in this huge city. We were church planters—it said so on our job description—but for the next months we struggled to meet people.

One morning in October, I saw an ad in the newspaper: "English professor wanted for adult evening school, David College." Since education in Hong Kong wasn't free, many young people never finished high school. Families faced heavy financial pressures, and thousands of students dropped out in their early teens. To support their families, they worked long hours for low pay at the colony's factories. Many so-called factories were more like warrens of one-room workshops operated out of people's bedrooms. Other factories were huge complexes. Yet, the Cantonese were renowned for their hard work and upward mobility. After several frustrating years in tedious factory conditions, many craved a better life. David College was one of many adult evening schools where motivated students could complete their high school education.

That evening I went to David College's address. The secretary introduced me to the headmaster, Mr. David Sham. In perfect, British-accented English, he asked, "What was your major field in college?"

Knowing that he was looking for an English major, I hesitated, but he pressed me for an answer. "Hebrew and Greek," I finally replied, knowing this would end the interview. We both had to smile, and Mr. Sham began to dismiss me, "I'm sorry, but we're looking for an English professor—"

Uncharacteristically, I interrupted: "Mr. Sham, it's true that I'm not an English major. But as a native English speaker I could be a real asset to your school. Let me tell you why I came to Kwun Tong. I am a Christian. I came here to meet young men and women to tell them about God's Son, Jesus Christ. I intend to start a church here."

Mr. Sham sat silently for many minutes, and I feared I had offended him. Finally, he looked up at me and spoke again: "Although I am not a Christian, my mother was a Christian, and every night we had prayer and Bible reading at the supper table. Mr. Ambacher, I think it would be good for you to come to our school. I hope you will not only teach the students English, but also give them the Gospel."

That morning, we hadn't known anyone in Kwun Tong except our new landlord, Mr. Chan, and we couldn't even talk with him. Now, I was an "English professor" in one of the largest secondary schools in all the area, with 500 evening school students and over 1,000 day school students. God was clearly heeding the prayers of all the faithful supporters we had visited on furlough. In the next years, we would settle in for the long-term, meeting students in the school and people in the community, and asking the Lord to open their hearts. First, however, I had to learn to teach English.

CALIFORNIA, U.S.A., JULY 15, 1971

"PRESIDENT RICHARD NIXON ANNOUNCED ON RADIO AND TELEVISION THAT
HE WOULD MAKE A PRESIDENTIAL VISIT TO CHINA BEFORE MAY 1972."

International Herald Tribune

CHAPTER 10

PROGRESS AND DISAPPOINTMENTS

I was nervous as I walked the few short blocks from our home to David College for my first night of teaching. My entrance to the Form 5 classroom (the British equivalent to eleventh grade) brought a murmur of surprise. *"Gwailo, gwailo!"* many called out. "A foreign ghost!" They obviously did not realize that I spoke Cantonese.

The room was filled with students in their late teens and early twenties. They drooped at their desks, weary after a long day at work. Many had not yet had their supper and would not eat until ten in the evening. But most were eager to learn and willing to try hard and then try again.

As I stepped to the front of the classroom, I looked over their faces. In the front row, Jimmy Chu gave me one of his perpetual smiles. Bonnie Leung perched pertly in her mini-skirt, and quiet Macky Wong hid in the very back seat. Chan Ping-fai, the class chairman, had an intent expression. Night after night, I would spend hours with these students, struggling through the intricacies and maddening inconsistencies of the English language. I desired to reach not only their minds, but their hearts. It was a daunting task, for what would be a daunting year, full of both progress and disappointments. Despite facing health troubles, natural disasters, car failures, and numerous other obstacles throughout the next term, Lyn and I would find Kwun Tong slowly opening to us.

Even though we had spent four years in Kowloon City, it was still difficult for Lyn to adjust to Kwun Tong, especially after returning from furlough in America, where she had luxuriated in the open space. Now she lived in a tiny apartment where the neighbors' windows were only a few feet away, where 5,000 people were packed into one acre. Later, she would call her struggle to adapt to this cramped lifestyle one of the major conflicts of her life. Thirsting for space, Lyn turned to the Lord for peace and determined to live by the life verses she had chosen while a student at the Omaha Baptist Bible Institute in Nebraska:

> If you extend your soul to the hungry
> And satisfy the afflicted soul,
> Then your light shall dawn in the darkness,
> And your darkness shall be as the noonday.
> The Lord will guide you continually,
> And satisfy your soul in drought,
> And strengthen your bones;
> You shall be like a watered garden,
> And like a spring of water, whose waters do not fail.
> (Isaiah 58:10–11)

Over the years, when we were desperate for escape from the relentless urban pressures, the Lord was our constant source of refreshment.

By Christmas 1970, we found we had come to prefer Kwun Tong to Kowloon City. As a self-contained satellite city, Kwun Tong felt more like a close-knit neighborhood, and less like a sprawling, impersonal city. While I developed relationships with my students at David College, Lyn was busy starting friendships with other women. She walked to the nearby local market to buy fruit and vegetables, smiling and chatting with everyone she met. Our children were swiftly growing and becoming part of the community. Kristi, now in sixth grade, was beginning the long struggle with braces on her teeth. Lori, in fifth grade, made friends with girls in the neighborhood. At age four, Brent started first grade in the British school system. A new member was added to the family when Brent managed to sneak a new kitten into the house over my protests.

In the spring of 1971, the Lord sent us another encouragement in the form of a new American family. Everett and Margaret Metzler, Mennonite missionaries with five children, moved into an apartment a few buildings away. Now we not only had new playmates for our children, but we were able to take turns driving the six miles to the British schools in Kowloon which our children attended. The trip usually took twenty-five minutes, but in heavy traffic and especially in heavy rain, the journey could easily take twice as long. We often sat at one major intersection, the Choi Hung circle, for long periods of time. As we waited, the children would suddenly call out, "Chinese Fire Drill!" Everyone would jump out of the car, run once around the car, and then jump back in. One night we crawled home through unusually heavy traffic. When we were still a mile from Kwun Tong, several of the children begged to get out of the car and race me home: they would walk, I would "drive." Of course, they arrived home first. Playfulness proved a way of relieving the frustration of the city's perpetual congestion.

* * *

As we prepared for church planting in Kwun Tong, Lyn and I searched for a Chinese coworker. While we were grateful for the work of the pioneer missionaries, it seemed to us that real growth could only begin when Chinese leaders became committed to reaching their own people. Wong Yee-shing, the son of the pastor of Evangel Baptist, our first rooftop church, seemed a fine candidate. Lyn and I had been among Yee-shing's teachers at HKBBI, and we knew he was more than merely intelligent. He also had a burden for lost people. He wanted to go as a missionary to another country in Southeast Asia, but decided that first he needed experience in helping to start a new church. After graduating with high honors from HKBBI, Yee-shing followed us to Kwun Tong. The Lord enabled us to locate a small apartment for rent across the street from our home, which we used both as a meeting place and as Yee-shing's quarters.

In January 1971, we initiated "Saturday Night Canteens," similar to the pattern we had used at Calvary Baptist in our first term, starting with table games, ping-pong, and refreshments. We distributed printed announcements in the neighborhood and at school. Other missionary friends came to help, playing the guitar, leading songs, and showing films. Ten young people came the first Saturday night, and attendance soon began to grow.

On the second Saturday night, however, during an especially vigorous game of ping-pong, Lyn tripped and fell to the floor. Her injuries seemed slight at first, but by the next morning, she was incapacitated by pain, unable to walk. At the Baptist Hospital in Kowloon, X-rays showed that she had cracked her coccyx, the small bone at the base of the spine. She spent five nights in the hospital and another week in bed at home, enduring the pain with her typical gentleness.

A few nights later, after evening school was over, the doorbell rang. I opened the door and was surprised to see a delegation of fifteen evening school students from David College bringing a basket of fruit for Lyn. Although Lyn's injury had been a great discouragement, and would prove to be only one of many calamities to befall her in the coming year, we were both encouraged by this display of kindness—evidence that we were making new friends in the community.

Despite Lyn's injury, attendance at the canteens climbed past thirty, and we started a weekly class, studying the evidences for Christian faith. We also started a Sunday night Bible study, to which I invited some of my students from David College, including Macky Wong, the shy inhabitant of the back row.

Macky was working in a factory, but hoped to leave soon for Scotland, where her older brother had a restaurant. She had studied in a Lutheran school, so she knew a little bit about the Bible, but nothing of a personal relationship with Christ. She was twenty, but very small and quiet. When she first visited our home, Macky was so painfully shy that Lyn predicted she would never return. Yet, she came for many weeks to our canteens and Bible studies. One night, after we had studied John 1:12—"But as many as received Him, to them He gave power to become the sons of God, even to them that believe on His name"—Macky Wong looked up and said very simply, "I believe."

A few days earlier, Macky and her friend Eva had visited our coworker in Kowloon, Carson Fremont. Macky was distraught because her visa to Scotland had been refused, and all her hopes of leaving Hong Kong and the grind of factory life seemed to have vanished. Carson clearly explained the plan of salvation to Macky and Eva, and they both received Jesus Christ. Now, in response to John 1:12, despite her fear of speaking aloud, Macky was testifying to her new faith. A few years later, Macky would enter HKBBI, her disappointment over the rejection of her visa application transformed into confidence that God must have a better plan for her life.

Lyn and I rejoiced in Macky's new faith, an affirmation that we were beginning to make progress in Kwun Tong. We already had the nucleus of an infant church. Yet, signs of progress were swiftly followed by hardships. In July 1971, after weeks of planning, we were excited to have prepared twelve campers from Kwun Tong to join Calvary Baptist Church for a week at summer camp. We had rented several cabins on an island in the New Territories. Some of our young people had taken a week's vacation from their jobs, and we thought they were ready for serious consideration of the Gospel. But Typhoon Rose, one of the worst typhoons in Hong Kong's history, swept across the colony with

120 mile per hour winds and torrential rain. Twenty-six inches of rain fell in three days.

At the same time, Lyn entered the hospital with pneumonia, and I drove back and forth to see her each day while the storm grew in intensity, my car shuddering in the winds. On Hong Kong Island, a six-story building slid down the slope of a high hill, crashing into a twelve-story building and knocking it over. Seventy-two people were killed. Just one block from our home in Kwun Tong, another hill collapsed. Many tons of dirt buried a community of squatter shacks under an avalanche of mud, killing seventy more. One of the girls who had been attending our canteen was missing, and with much trepidation, I went to watch as workers dug out bodies, praying that hers would not be among them. I was appalled by the utter devastation, the mud-drenched corpses and flattened homes. Thankfully, the girl was later found alive, but so many others were not. Typhoon Rose knocked out electricity in all of Kowloon and the New Territories for several days.

To our great disappointment, we were forced to cancel our camp program. When calm returned, we drove around the neighborhood, surveying the damage. Telephone wires hung to the ground, tangled and warped. Debris filled the streets—twisted branches of trees, mangled tin roofs of shacks, trashed remains of furniture. Kwun Tong looked as if it had been transformed back into the garbage dump it had once been.

Lyn recovered from pneumonia, only to enter the Baptist Hospital again in August for minor surgery. She was only supposed to stay overnight, but she developed a severe reaction to the spinal anesthetic. The hospital put her on IVs and morphine, and she lay, barely conscious, in grave jeopardy. I was left to cope on my own, struggling to manage the household and watch after the children, deeply anxious for her safety. Fellow ABWE missionaries Margaret Paswaters and Darline Fremont helped care for our children, and Pat Henry gave me cooking tips, unstopping the sink after I clogged it with grease. I went to the hospital day after day, but there was little change. Lyn lost fifteen pounds and grew weaker every day. The surgeon, our good friend Don Langford, warned me, "If we cannot get her turned around, we are going to lose her."

Every night, as I drove the six miles from the Baptist Hospital in Kowloon Tong back to Kwun Tong, I tried not to give way to the gnawing fear that gripped me. Lyn was not only the center of my life and the heartbeat of our family, she was also the magnet that attracted young people to our work. I knew that I could not live without her, and that we could not survive in Kwun Tong without her.

Suddenly, for no discernible reason, Lyn began to recover. She was finally able to come home after her unexpected ten-day "vacation." My relief was almost inexpressible. We were deeply grateful to God, and realized more than ever the frailty of our lives and our complete dependence on Him for our safety and health.

Our encounters with sickness and disaster were not yet over. When Lyn was told she needed to have her gallbladder removed, we scheduled a mid-term vacation in Baguio City. There, in the clear air and open mountains of the Philippines, we thought Lyn might better recover after surgery. But another fierce typhoon brought rain, floods, and landslides to the Philippines. At the airport in Baguio, one end of the runway simply slid down the mountainside.

"Now what does God have in mind for us? He must be trying to tell us something. Should we just unpack and stay home?" asked Kristi.

Instead of leaving the country, we rented a room at the Dragon Inn in the New Territories. It was so small that three of us had to sleep on the floor. Yet, we enjoyed our holiday, playing badminton, riding bikes, indulging in good Chinese food and terrible French toast, and spending hours in the swimming pool. At the end, we returned to Kwun Tong refreshed and ready to resume work.

By September 1972, more than twenty people, most in their teens and twenties, regularly attended Saturday night canteen, and a similar number came for Sunday night Bible study. But it was one thing to play ping-pong and watch Christian movies, quite another to seriously consider the Lordship of Christ. Once again, we planned a weekend camp where students would be confronted with a clear presentation of the Gospel. We rented a campsite in the New Territories not far from the border with Communist China. Bill Reid joined us with friends from his new church plant, Faith Baptist Church of Happy Valley on Hong Kong Island. After Joan's death almost three years earlier, Bill had remained in Hong Kong and continued his work. Now, he was beginning to see some young people coming to Christ in Happy Valley.

In the weeks leading up to the camp, we specifically asked God to give us young people who would clearly declare their allegiance to Jesus Christ. The entire field council joined us in prayer for weeks before camp. Plans were made and carefully coordinated: what food to buy, which campers needed to be transported and at which times. Then, just three days before camp, my Volkswagen van developed problems. I rushed it to the garage and, explaining the urgency of the Friday afternoon camp, I pleaded with the mechanic to have it ready by Thursday.

"I'll try," he answered, "but Mr. Ambacher, your car is very sick!"

I picked up the repaired car on Friday, just six hours before camp. As I roared impatiently from the garage, I was reviewing all the duties ahead—what things to pack, what to do first—when I noticed the car was almost out of gas. I tried to think of the nearest gas station, but in land-scarce Hong Kong, stations were few and far between. I was in the unfamiliar Wong Tai Sin area and couldn't figure out where to turn when I heard an ominous cough.

Surrounded on all sides by vehicles on a crowded street, my car ran out of gas. Dozens of cars began honking behind me, and I had no idea what to do.

As I jumped out of the car, I prayed just one sentence: "Lord, you *have* to help me now!" I started to run. At the corner I paused and turned right, although I wasn't sure it was the best direction. One block away, I ran almost directly into Bob Paswaters' car.

"Bob, what are you doing here?" I practically shouted. "You don't know where I can get a can of gas, do you?"

Bob smiled and reached behind the seat, "I just happen to have a can of gas right here."

I took the can and ran back to my car. In a matter of minutes, I was on my way again. Comparing notes with Bob and the other missionaries later, I found that Bob had not been in that part of the city for many months. I also discovered that he was the only one of our missionaries who regularly carried a can of gas in his car. As I started driving again, a surge of excitement swept over me. The Holy Spirit was clearly caring for every detail of the weekend camp. I couldn't wait to get there and see what else He was going to do.

On Friday evening, fifty-one campers registered, including thirty-one from Kwun Tong. We had four simple but direct messages: What is sin? How did God reveal Himself? Who was Jesus Christ? How can we be saved? On Sunday morning, seven of our Kwun Tong campers stood to indicate they wanted to follow Jesus. God had given us the breakthrough we so desperately needed.

We began a program of systematic follow-up. Since the weekend camp had proved so successful, we began to plan others, joining with Faith Baptist and Heritage Baptist, the Paswaters' new church in Mei Foo. At the Christmas 1972 camp, over 100 campers attended in weather just a few degrees above freezing. We shivered in unheated cabins and shower rooms. For the next four years, despite all kinds of weather and hardships, we never held a weekend camp without a student making a public confession of faith in Christ.

Miriam Yuen, whom we had originally contacted through an ad in the pen pal page of the local newspaper, the *South China Morning Post,* came one Sunday night after Bible study and asked, "How long must I wait before I can receive God's love?" Lyn helped her to pray and become a new child of God.

Each new confession of faith brought Lyn and me great joy. But as we became more involved in the lives of our neighbors and students, we also saw more clearly the painful effects of sin and poverty on their lives. May Lai (not her real name) was one woman to whom we tried to reach out in compassion. She had left an unhappy marriage in Singapore and brought her two daughters with her to Hong Kong to start over. Without arranging for an official divorce, she married another man in Hong Kong. They had a son, but the couple fought constantly.

One night when I returned home from teaching, Lyn met me at the door of our apartment. She put her finger over her lips to motion me to be quiet. "May Lai is here," she said. Just a few hours before I arrived, May Lai's second husband had tried to stab her. Lyn and I kept the distraught May Lai and her children for several days in our apartment, which seemed to shrink each day.

The evening after she moved in, I recognized her husband's voice when I answered the phone. "I know my wife is living with you," he growled, "and I am going to stab you to death."

A few days later, several police officers came to our apartment and asked May Lai to go with them to the station and make a statement. She told me she was scared, so I went with her. The officers agreed to let her return to our home as soon as she had completed her statement, and I left the police station. But while we were eating supper, May Lai phoned. In a frightened voice she cried, "They are trying to force me to go home with my husband."

I knew he could kill her, and I raced to the Kwun Tong Police Station. "I'm here to get May Lai," I said.

"She's not here," the sergeant lied.

I walked past the barrier and started down the hall.

"You can't go back there," he said.

"I'm going to look in every office until I find her," I answered, throwing the first office door open for effect.

"Wait here, I'll bring her out," he answered.

As I drove home with May Lai, I was shaking. Though she became our close friend, May Lai remained cool to the Gospel, and her family life stayed in shambles. Within a few days, she moved back home, and eventually she returned to Singapore. Church planting brought joys, but it also brought sadness when people rejected the Gospel. God did not always permit us to see change in the lives of the people we reached out to.

* * *

The more we became involved in the community, the more our hearts were burdened for the thousands of factory workers in Kwun Tong who labored at menial tasks for low wages. The economic prosperity of Hong Kong, as the colony grew closer to becoming one of the three top financial districts in the world, was built on the backs of the factory workers. For women, the responsibility of supporting their families was especially heavy. Many could barely earn enough to support their children, and whole families crowded into single-room apartments in the housing estates. The tedious conditions of factory work led to a high turnover rate. The factory workers yearned for the chance to be educated, earn a better wage, and change their status in life.

In August 1973, an exciting opportunity opened for Lyn. Fairchild Semi-Conductor Factory in Kwun Tong, which employed over 2,000 women, took a survey to see what extra-curricular activities they could provide to make their workers happier, hoping to reduce the too-frequent turnover. The women overwhelmingly requested English classes. Lyn was invited to teach two classes, one to afternoon shift workers before they started work, and the other to morning shift workers who had just finished. After slowly winning their confidence and friendship, Lyn brought some of the girls to Sunday night Bible study. Once again, education had opened doors to evangelism. The English language had proved to be a commodity that we could trade across cultures in exchange for the opportunity to share our faith.

But we still faced cultural challenges when we went to the local swimming pool. Brent and his fellow MK, John Fremont, were mobbed by dozens of Chinese children who wanted to touch their white-blond hair. We no longer sensed the simmering animosity towards foreigners that had characterized Hong Kong during the 1967 riots; instead, the problem was an over-abundance of curiosity. As outsiders, we were objects of fascination, and the boys could not get a peaceful moment to swim. A Scottish friend from language school, Billy Campbell, invited us to the Kowloon Cricket Club.

Cricket clubs were peculiarly reminiscent of the British influence in Hong Kong; in every British colony, the British inevitably congregated at clubs where they could practice their familiar customs. Such clubs were like faithful re-creations of England, islands within the larger culture of the colony. We were initially concerned that the Kowloon Cricket Club (KCC), like many other British clubs at the time, would bar Chinese from membership. We had come to Hong Kong to reach out to the Chinese, not to exclude them from our privileges. However, the KCC was different from other clubs in that it allowed Chinese members, so we joined. The British club proved a place where cultures blended—we Americans often invited our Chinese friends for dinner and swimming. Although I never took up cricket myself, in future years, my son, Brent, did learn to play at his school.

In 1973, we looked back over the last challenging years. Despite the difficulty of returning from furlough only to move to a new city, our children had adjusted well to life in Kwun Tong. Kristi was now attending the British middle school, King George V, tearing through stacks of homework, practicing the piano, and reluctantly visiting the orthodontist. Lori, always artistic, began writing stories, making paper dolls, and assembling collections of all kinds of objects. Brent became my sparring partner, teased his big sisters, and demonstrated his growing scientific bent as he pored over encyclopedias, especially articles about engines and parts of the human body. Though Lyn had struggled through one illness after another, God had preserved her from more serious harm and blessed her relationships with the Chinese. Lyn's life verses had come to serve for both of us as we reached out to the students and factory workers of Hong Kong.

Though we had known no one when we first came to Kwun Tong three years earlier, God was clearly helping us to connect to people. As we learned to extend our souls to the hungry, God solved our own afflictions. When we encountered the darkness of disappointment, we remembered the promise of Isaiah 58: "Then shall your light dawn in the darkness, and your darkness shall be as the noonday." Our new believers—Macky, Eva, Miriam Yeung, and many others—were certainly evidence of light in darkness. In retrospect, the natural disasters, sicknesses, and small catastrophes that once seemed like dragons raising their heads now seemed powerless to completely halt our work.

BEIJING AIRPORT, CHINA, FEBRUARY 21, 1972

"PRESIDENT RICHARD NIXON STEPPED ON THE TARMAC THIS MORNING
AND PUBLICLY SHOOK HANDS WITH THE WAITING PREMIER CHOU EN-LAI.
THERE WAS ONLY A SMALL LINE OF CHINESE OFFICIALS, AND THE MOTORCADE
TO THE GUESTHOUSE, DRIVING DOWN EMPTY STREETS, WAS SHOWN LIVE
ON TELEVISION IN HONG KONG."

Jonathan Spence, The Search for Modern China

CHAPTER 11

NEW STRATEGIES FOR A NEW DECADE

Historian Jonathan Spence characterizes the 1972 talks between Mao Tse-tung and President Nixon as "cautious and elliptical," but suggests that, nonetheless, they marked a turning point in China's foreign relations.[1] During the 1960s, amid the horrors of the Cultural Revolution, the rulers of the Communist Party had turned their backs on the West. But in the 1970s, they would begin to ease the doors open again, looking for new strategies to define the economy and spur growth in China. By the end of the 1970s, "elliptical" talks would make way for more robust relations. In a way, our work in Hong Kong followed a similar pattern. By 1973, the Lord had given us a small foothold in Kwun Tong.

But progress was slow—three years to gather thirty regular attendees—and if we followed the rate of growth of earlier ABWE church plants in Hong Kong, it would take years before an independent, indigenous church would be established. With the satellite cities mushrooming at fantastic rates, Lyn and I wondered if we needed better methods of church planting. In the years between 1964 and 1970, seventeen new missionaries had arrived to work with the ABWE team in Hong Kong, eight couples and one single woman. They were young, enthusiastic, and open to innovative ways of taking the Gospel to the Chinese people. Lyn and I observed as two of these couples, Bob and Margaret Paswaters and Bill and Sharon Commons, began to implement new strategies for church planting.

Bob and Margaret had arrived on the mission field one year before us, in 1964. Like all new missionaries, they spent their first term learning Cantonese and helping in existing churches. Then, in 1971, they learned that Mobil Oil Corporation was building a large private housing development called Mei Foo, or "Beautiful and Prosperous New Village," on the waterfront west of Kowloon. The new city would be mammoth, with a planned population of 80,000. I had found a way to start relationships in Kwun Tong by entering David College as an English teacher; Bob and Margaret took the idea of education a step further and opened their own kindergarten on the second floor of one of the buildings in Mei Foo.

Believing that excellence in their school would be a good witness, Bob and Margaret were committed to providing the highest-quality facilities for the children. They spent months poring over plans, selecting furniture, and supervising the interior construction of the kindergarten and church area. Margaret designed distinctive red and white uniforms for the new pupils. From a starting enrollment of 250, the school swiftly grew to 640 students in two sessions. A staff of sixteen teachers kept the school running smoothly. This commitment to the children gained the attention of the children's parents. Students were taught Bible along with other subjects, and soon not only students but also their parents began to attend Sunday school. Bob and Margaret founded Heritage Baptist Church from this group of believers and held services in the kindergarten auditorium on Saturdays and Sundays. Heritage Baptist in Mei Foo grew faster than any other ABWE church in Hong Kong up to that time. During its first year, 1972, the church averaged sixty-six in morning worship services.

Bill and Sharon Commons, like Bob and Margaret Paswaters, realized that fulfilling social needs—whether for education or social service centers—provided an immediate entrance into the community. Bill and Sharon, who had arrived in 1967, shared the field council's concern for the satellite cities and were particularly interested in the second city, Tsuen Wan, even farther to the west of Kowloon.

While researching Tsuen Wan, Bill found that several other mission agencies had planted churches in the new government housing estates by starting youth and social service centers. He discovered that if a mission or church were willing to operate a youth center, a children's center, or a center for retired people, the Hong Kong government would lease the space without charging rent. Once again, the Hong Kong government's willingness to work with missionaries proved a blessing, as did, ironically, the restrictions on space.

By the 1970s, the British government was committed to the housing and resettlement projects and searched for any efficient means to improve the quality of life within the new housing estates. The Hong Kong resettlement projects would be held up as an example throughout the world, especially when the British justified their continuing presence in the colony.

Requiring agencies starting service centers to complete the construction of the premises proved an expedient way for the government to save money. The new buildings resembled empty, concrete shells and required windows, finished floors, plastered walls, wiring, plumbing, and painting. Bill Commons carefully worked out the costs of finishing one facility and starting a center, and his plan was quickly approved by the Hong Kong Field Council.

In the fall of 1972, the government leased us almost 6,000 square feet of space, divided into nine bays, on the ground floor of Block 12 of the Kwai Shing Housing Estate. Kwai Shing was a new section of Tsuen Wan and was projected to have a population of 83,000 when completed. In November 1972, under Bill and Sharon's direction, the Kwai Shing Christian Social Service Center and Kwai Shing Baptist Church opened.

By understanding the Chinese culture, Bill and Sharon were able to offer programs that would appeal directly to them. During the week, the service center held programs to attract people from the community, daily children's clubs, typing classes, English conversation classes, first-aid and health classes, a guitar club, Chinese medicine classes, and Bible classes. I also helped at the Kwai Shing center, driving across the city on Monday nights to teach the Gospel of Mark to a group of teenagers who were not yet Christians. Some of these students, such as Richard Kwok and Donna Tong, would become some of the first Christians in the Kwai Shing church. I was thrilled to experience the center's progress firsthand.

The original social service center staff was made up of four full-time workers. One was Bonnie Leung, one of the first Christians to attend our Kwun Tong services. She was the vivacious, unusually pretty nineteen-year-old whom I had met at David College in my first year. Bonnie had been a typical evening student, struggling to escape the factory life. As a small girl, she had helped her mother assemble plastic flowers in their one-room home. After she finished sixth grade, she had sacrificed her education to work in a garment factory, starting at age twelve, so her older brother and younger brothers and sisters could continue their studies.

Before she came to our Kwun Tong church, Bonnie and her best friend, Eva, had attended a Christian and Missionary Alliance chapel, where they decided to follow Christ. When we met Bonnie, her life showed little evidence of any change, but as the months went by, she began to show understanding and great interest in the Word of God. Lyn helped her with English and, in return, Bonnie helped Lyn prepare Sunday school lessons in Cantonese. Bonnie began witnessing to her classmates. She longed for a more fulfilling job, but with her limited education the possibilities seemed slim.

Then Bonnie told us that she was moving to join her family in a new government housing estate in Kwai Shing. We immediately recommended her to Bill and Sharon as a worker in their new center. Though we would miss her deeply, we were glad she would be with her family, who certainly needed Christ. Bonnie worked hard for Bill and Sharon, and proved to be especially gifted in handling children and young people. Lyn used to remark that Bonnie "loved them into the kingdom of God."

In addition to Bonnie, Bill was able to secure Yeung Po-wan, a 1969 graduate of HKBBI, as the regular Sunday preacher for the new Kwai Shing Baptist Church. Po-wan had been pastoring at Sunshine Baptist for four years. He now agreed to join the Commonses to help pioneer the new work at Kwai Shing. As became increasingly the pattern in ABWE's work in Hong Kong, the involvement of nationals in leadership led to significant growth. As Lyn and I prepared for our 1974 furlough, Kwai Shing was already averaging forty in Sunday services.

Lyn and I began to pray about using Bill's and Sharon's new strategies to expand our work in Kwun Tong. But we were already short of personnel—Bonnie had left to join the Commonses, and our Kwun Tong coworker, Wong Yee-shing, had concluded that his skills did not lie in church planting. He started a Sunday school in 1972 and spent time visiting the homes of the students, but, in 1973, he left Kwun Tong to join the staff at Sunshine Baptist Church and to head up the library at HKBBI.

Worse yet, the field council was confronting an impending furlough crisis. In June 1973, four of the eight ABWE missionary families in Hong Kong would depart on furlough, leaving six churches and the Bible institute in the care of the remaining four families. Lyn and I would have to lead Bill Reid's Faith Baptist

Church on Hong Kong Island, in addition to the Kwun Tong work. We didn't know how we would have time to manage both responsibilities, much less implement new strategies.

Then God sent an unanticipated solution and blessing. Lyn's parents, Fred and Anne Alexander, recently retired from a life in the pastorate, suddenly decided to come to Hong Kong. Since they had a retirement income, and could live in the apartment where Wong Yee-shing had lived, they would not need monthly support. They arrived from Savannah, Ohio, on August 6. They loved their little flat, which needed very little housework. Though they were used to wide, open country, they adjusted surprisingly well to the noise and the teeming crowds.

For the next year, we were blessed to work side by side. Lyn was overjoyed to have her parents so near, and the Alexanders were delighted to be with their grandchildren. "Grampy and Grammy" Alexander, as the students called them, took over much of the work at Faith Baptist. They led English classes in Kwun Tong and spent hours talking and counseling with young people. The Alexanders' "grey heads" gave them a special connection to the students, for in Chinese culture the elderly are treated with great respect. The students cherished the wisdom of the Alexanders, who were delighted in turn to be so useful.

In 1974, as Lyn and I planned our furlough, the Alexanders decided to stay in Hong Kong a second year. With their help, enough support was provided to resolve the personnel crisis. A Chinese couple from Calvary Baptist Church, Daniel and Patricia Tse, took over the preaching at Kwun Tong. Fred Alexander covered the preaching at Faith Baptist, and our coworker Bob Henry volunteered to serve as an advisor to both churches.

Bob and his wife, Pat, were experienced church planters, helping to start three churches in their nine years in Hong Kong. A few years later, they would leave Hong Kong to establish a media center at the ABWE office in Cherry Hill, New Jersey.

Using new techniques in slides, video, and digital imaging, Bob would help missionaries produce outstanding presentations on missions. Over the next twenty-two years, an estimated 500,000 people would view Bob's presentations in churches and schools throughout North America. For now, however, we were confident that the churches were safe in their capable hands. Pat was a sensitive, caring person, a close friend of Lyn's, and Bob had the valuable trait of being able to work behind the scenes, not caring if he was in the limelight.

We were free to leave for our second furlough in June 1974, secure in our knowledge that the Hong Kong churches were being looked after. As we flew back to the United States with our children, we were already wondering what direction our work would take when we returned for our third term. Our hearts were still in Kwun Tong, and we yearned to reach the huge remaining population of the city.

BEIJING, CHINA, 1975

"A Beijing radio station began broadcasting
English-language lessons again.
For the first time since 1966,
China sent students abroad."

Philip Short, Mao: A Life

CHAPTER 12

ACCEPTING A CHALLENGE

During the furlough before our third term in 1975, Lyn and I looked forward to implementing new strategies in our work in Kwun Tong. However, before we finished our furlough, the Hong Kong Baptist Bible Institute was left without a director. Our new challenge would be to find a way to manage two responsibilities at once.

The Lord had led Don Trott to remain in the United States, and though Bill Reid, the original founder of the HKBBI, had returned to Hong Kong, he had recently remarried and did not want to return as director. Bill and his new wife, Gloria, settled back into the work at Faith Baptist Church.

The Bible institute, which was so crucial to discipleship and training of the new Chinese believers, was hampered by the lack of continuity in leadership. Furthermore, the institute badly needed permanent premises. When money-hungry landlords evicted the school from rented flats twice in two years, the number of students dwindled.

Earlier, in 1970, and on short notice, ABWE missionary Carson Fremont had become the school's third president. Carson had served in the Baptist Bible Seminary in Manila for over ten years, including a short period as president. In 1964, Carson, Darline, and their children had transferred to Hong Kong. Carson's skills lay in teaching, not administration, and he reluctantly accepted the leadership of the school. We admired Carson's selfless commitment to the difficult and sometimes thankless task of administration.

In 1972, Carson located a flat in Kowloon, just one-half mile from Nathan Road, and a central location for bus routes. The field council agreed with Carson's plan to purchase the apartment, and thus secure a permanent location for HKBBI. Carson had solved one of HKBBI's needs, but he made it clear to the ABWE Board that he did not wish to continue as the president of the school. From 1972 to 1975, HKBBI had no full-time students, and only evening classes continued. Members in our ABWE churches began to wonder if HKBBI's future was in peril.

The ABWE Board turned to Lyn and me to fill the gap, asking us to become involved in HKBBI. The Hong Kong missionaries knew that without a healthy school we would all be continually hampered by the lack of trained Chinese leaders. While Lyn and I were still praying about our decision, the Board appointed me as the fourth president of the Bible institute, and I accepted, making it clear that our Kwun Tong church would remain an important part of our work.

As I contemplated the daunting new responsibility, I decided to pursue further study to prepare for leadership of the institute. I had not been involved in formal study since graduating from seminary more than ten years before. I felt that I needed the discipline of a formal program and the give-and-take of the classroom situation to sharpen my mind again. I asked the advice of Harold Amstutz, ABWE's deputation director, who was enrolled in the Doctor of Ministry program at Western Conservative Baptist Seminary in Portland, Oregon. Harold suggested entering the program at Western, and appreciating Harold's keen mind and preaching ability, I enrolled.

It seemed to be just the course I was looking for, because the program was designed for Christian workers who could sharpen their tools while remaining in their work. I took the first two core courses in the summer of 1975 and flew back from Hong Kong for two more courses during the summer of 1976. It was exciting to be on campus again, and the classes proved to be the stimulating experience I had been looking for.

But there were some uneasy moments as a man educated in the 1950s plunged into the academic world of the 1970s. Exposure to new concepts can be challenging. At Western, the most important lesson was from Luke 6:40, the need to train disciples. That verse became an inspiration to me, as I realized that I needed not merely to lead Hong Kong people to Christ, I needed to commit myself to seeing them built up. When a student is fully trained, he *will* resemble his teacher.

My classes strengthened my resolve to emphasize discipleship training when I returned to Hong Kong. During furlough, Lyn and I spent much time in prayer, asking the Lord to prepare us for the challenges ahead and requesting our supporting churches to continue as our prayer partners.

We also left a special prayer request with our supporters. We had already experienced the incredible traffic congestion described in the *Guinness Book of Records:* "In Hong Kong . . . if all the cars and buses were on the road simultaneously there would be only eight yards, one foot, eleven inches between vehicles."[1] So we asked all our friends to pray that we would be able to find a parking place to rent for our car. It was often impossible to park in Kwun Tong, and parking violation tickets were quite common. On the return from our previous furlough, God had blessed our prayers to find an apartment. Based on the way He had met our needs in the past, we were confident that He would again provide.

* * *

We flew out of Seattle late on August 24, 1975, on a jumbo jet with every seat filled—a stark contrast to the empty freighter in which we had arrived the first time. After a four-hour flight to Alaska, and a refueling stop, we flew ten hours non-stop to Hong Kong. The landing was always dramatic—coming through the long, narrow corridor between the mountains, we circled and landed in a sharp turn over the hills that guarded the crowded city.

It was early in the morning when we arrived to begin our third term in the Crown Colony. When we opened the morning papers, the *South China Morning Post* reported: "The Greater Kwun Tong area has a population of 480,000 in 10 housing estates alone and an overall population of 600,000. In 15 years this district has grown from a rubbish dump to a manufacturing colossus with an output exceeding that of half the countries in the United Nations."[2]

This manufacturing colossus was the city we returned to. We had only been away for a year, but we were appalled by the noise, the dirt, the smells, and the dense traffic. Living in Kwun Tong had always been a matter of endurance and acclimation. Even I, who loved cities, felt initially exhausted each time I returned. Construction, airport, traffic, industrial, and human noise made Hong Kong one of the noisiest cities on earth, worse even than New York, Tokyo, or London. Even when not working, it was difficult to relax, for every place in the city—parks, tea houses, restaurants, shops—was always full of people. Everyone always seemed to be hurrying to an appointment. Because the government had been set on two main objectives, economic growth and housing resettlements, very little had been done to protect the environment. Hong Kong grew so swiftly that its seas and rivers were polluted, and the traffic density meant that lead emissions were being pumped into the air.[3]

But we had adjusted to these pitfalls of urban life, and we would do so again. It was harder to accept the skyrocketing crime rate that, according to police maps, centered in our satellite city. The crime rate jumped 76 percent in three years, with violent crimes soaring twenty-fold over the last decade. A few days after our return, three gang leaders chased a teenaged newspaper vendor who had not been willing to pay protection money, catching him in front of our apartment building and stabbing out his eye. Lyn and I wondered once more if we were right to bring our children to live in Kwun Tong.

Just at this time, God encouraged our hearts with His specific answer to our prayer. A parking space became available right next door to our apartment building. We heralded this as a special foretaste of what God would do for us during the next four-year term. Despite our reservations about city-living, Lyn and the children were happy to be back in the increasingly familiar Kwun Tong. Vegetable and fruit vendors greeted Lyn by name when she walked down the street. Caesar, the kitten Brent had smuggled into the apartment, seemed as pleased as a cat could admit to be at our return—and was fast becoming fat and sassy. We realized Kwun Tong had truly become our home.

Our family, always close, enjoyed many special holidays, or "hols," as the kids called them at their British school. Christmas was a particularly magical time. Lyn and I took the children shopping for presents, visiting the gaily decorated British department store, Lane Crawford's, which was lit up like a British version of Macy's, and lunching in their tearoom. While the children were in school, Lyn and I went on dates, strolling together beneath the bright lights of the Central District on Hong Kong Island, simply enjoying each other's company.

The children flourished in Hong Kong. The colony was their home; it was where they came alive. However, the kids sometimes made our hearts stop with their daring, especially Brent, who seemed completely lacking in fear. On the last morning of a weekend canoe camp in the rugged Sai Kung Peninsula in the New Territories, we suddenly realized that nine-year-old Brent and his pal John Fremont were missing. We discovered they had taken a canoe and were already out in the ocean, far out of sight.

Chan Ping-fai, the same believer who had escaped from China by swimming, swam out to find them. He must have known he could swim for mile after mile. We watched as he grew smaller in the distance and finally disappeared. After what seemed like an eternity, the canoe came in sight, with Chan Ping-fai and the two boys aboard. While we were trying to decide whether to hug the boys or spank them, Brent called out across the water, "Dad, we saved Chan Ping-fai!"

* * *

Shortly before our return from furlough, a typical summer typhoon had hit Hong Kong. The first time I returned to the Hong Kong Baptist Bible Institute to take up my new assignment, I was greeted by a broken window, with tiles floating on the water that covered the floor. I looked at the ironic sign on the door: "President's Office."

After cleaning up the office, I set out to develop an internship program for the school. I could still remember how thrilled we were to see the first three graduates leave our school in 1969 and 1970. But I could also remember the puzzlement we felt when two of them resigned from their first pastorates and all expressed a feeling of inadequacy. We had given them book knowledge, but had we really prepared them for the work of the ministry?

The Bible tells us that the disciples stayed with Christ for three years. A. B. Bruce points out that they entered into an apprenticeship or internship: "They were to learn, in the privacy of an intimate daily fellowship with their Master, what they should do, believe and teach. The training of these men was to be a constant and prominent part of Christ's personal work."[4]

So we required students to have weekend internship involvements in church plants. On weekends, all of the students would work side by side with one of the other teachers or me, acting out the very principles we had spent the week teaching them. Later, the greatest success of the school would be attributed to our insistence that students put theory into practice in our internship program.

In 1975, we developed a ten-year plan for the Bible institute to address the obvious need for more students. The plan featured three objectives for the next decade: to recruit more students, to find good Chinese teachers who were involved in church planting, and to search for a larger location for the school. We started developing more attractive classes, and I visited each of ABWE's seven churches to challenge prospective students.

Leading the institute and our fledgling church in Kwun Tong simultaneously was less of a burden than I might have expected. Though I did not know it then, my temporary leadership of HKBBI would become permanent, and I would lead the school until 1996. I worked long hours at HKBBI during the week, yet I found that my work at the institute fed my work in church planting. Unlike many academics, I was greatly blessed to have the opportunity both to teach theory and to put it into practice.

In Kwun Tong, the small nucleus of believers was almost ready to call a Chinese pastor and organize into a local church. We were amazed by the contrast with our arrival five years before, when we didn't know a single person in the huge satellite city. Now, we spent time teaching the believers, and resuming outreach strategies that had been successful in the past. Lyn returned to the Fairchild Factory to teach English classes, and we restarted the popular weekend camps. During 1976, two different groups were baptized in the South China Sea. Rose Lam, who was baptized that summer, sent us a card:

> For my baptism—thank you for giving me the words,
> Thank you for praying for me,
> Thank you for sharing the pleasure and pains,
> Thank you for leading me back to the Christ home.
> A thousand thanks that I cannot explain.
> I will only pray for you.

As our church grew, our children grew as well. Kristi, in Form 6 (roughly equivalent to a high school senior), was chosen as editor of the yearbook at King George V School, which had over 1,000 students. She was also secretary of the city's Christian Youth Fellowship. Lori, the equivalent of a high school junior, received five prizes on the school's Speech Day and finished first in her class in seven of nine exams. Displaying his usual aptitude for sports, Brent played "ruggers" (rugby) and soccer in seventh grade.

At King George V, our children were learning to be truly multicultural citizens. The kids had classmates from over forty countries and, at the dinner table every night, imitating different accents became a favorite activity. "Lori," Kristi would announce, "you're Indian tonight." Kristi would be Scottish, Brent would be African or Chinese, and the kids would converse with each other, erupting into giggles as they tried out scraps of other languages and tried to capture their friends' exact tones.

In accordance with British tradition, Speech Day was always a gala occasion at King George V. Half the school's 1,000 students and parents attended the evening program, designed to highlight the musical, oratorical, and artistic skills of the students. Our three children often sang in the school choir or played in the orchestra. An unfortunate circumstance occurred one Speech Day, however, on the night Lori played viola in the orchestra. While we mingled with other parents after the program, drinking hot tea on the cold November evening, Lori went outside to put her viola in our Toyota van. The car was locked, so she put the instrument under the car where no one would see it.

When it was time to go home, I went to get the car so the family would not have to walk in the cold. When it dawned on Lori where I was going, she ran after me. But it was too late. Just as I reversed the car to turn around, I heard two sounds almost simultaneously: Lori's anguished cry, "Dad!" and the awful crunch of the viola under the wheels of the car. We kissed Lori's tears away and tried to assure her that our pride in her accomplishments was worth much more than the cost of replacing the school's viola.

In 1977, our children unexpectedly gained two brothers for a time. They were cousins of Yoe Sim Kwan, who had been a Red Guard in China's Cultural Revolution in the 1960s. While marching in a parade in Beijing, she prayed that if God existed, He would show Himself to her. She came to Hong Kong but, although she was a chemistry teacher, Hong Kong did not recognize her credentials. She answered an ad for household help, working for the Reids. Rebecca Reid led her to the Lord.

When she found a teaching job, Sim Kwan moved to Kowloon and began to attend our Sunday evening services in Kwun Tong. Because of the turmoil in the killing fields of their native Cambodia, several of Sim Kwan's cousins came to Hong Kong. Three of them began to attend on Sunday nights with her. Their situation was bleak. Because they spoke Cambodian and not Cantonese, they had little prospect of fitting into Hong Kong society. Against all of our advice and pleading, Benjamin, the eldest, returned to Cambodia to see his family. He was brutally killed in Phnom Penh. When we heard no news of Benjamin for several months, Lyn was convinced that we should take the other two boys into our home, teach them English, and try to find a home for them in the United States.

They moved in with their few possessions, and Lyn promptly dubbed them Joseph and Daniel, "after two other exiles from home." Brent was thrilled to suddenly have two older brothers, and the boys made progress with English. Lyn asked friends to pray that God would clearly lead the boys to a new home.

The answer came unexpectedly after Lyn sent a tape to her brother, Paul, who pastored Westminster Presbyterian Church in Huntsville, Alabama. Paul wrote back:

> Lyn, you have become the first woman preacher to hold forth in a Reformed Presbyterian church. I played excerpts from your tape this past Wednesday night, including the entire section on the Cambodians, Joseph and Daniel. Our elders are still a little reluctant about ordaining you to the office of teaching elder, but your sermon was nevertheless quite effective. It appears that we have two or three families who are serious about wanting to take Joseph and Daniel into their homes.

Paul and Lyn eagerly attacked the red tape on both sides of the Pacific, and on September 1, 1977, we received the happy cable: "Joseph, Daniel arrived safely in Huntsville. We are pleased. Praise the Lord. Pray for us. Paul Alexander."

Phil and Karen Olin adopted Joseph, and Daniel went to live with their neighbors Fred and Emma Peace. The boys attended Westminster Academy in Huntsville, and both came to know the Lord. Today they have happy Christian families, with Joseph Lo living in Vancouver, Washington, and Daniel Lo in Norwalk, California.

Thus far in our third term, God had blessed us—allowing us to see both our children and our church grow and flourish, enabling me to assume the leadership of HKBBI, providing homes for Daniel and Joseph, and giving us the peace and strength to readapt to the challenges of life in hectic Kwun Tong. But as we surveyed Kwun Tong, our hearts continued to be burdened by the need to expand our outreach strategies and turn over the church to Chinese leadership. Already, it was outgrowing both our home and our guidance. Lyn crystallized our thoughts in a letter to friends in the United States:

We didn't choose to live in Kwun Tong for its scenery, or cultural advantages, or conveniences. There really isn't much here to excite a sightseer, unless people excite you. We came to Kwun Tong because we believed God wanted us to tell the Good News and to establish a church. Now our apartment is too small for the size of our group. We wonder what the Lord has in mind for the future of our group of believers and further outreach into this city.

BEIJING, CHINA, SEPTEMBER 9, 1976, 12:10 A.M.

"BARELY TWO MONTHS AFTER ONE OF THE WORST EARTHQUAKES
IN CHINA'S RECORDED HISTORY, CHAIRMAN MAO TSE-TUNG DIED
OF COMPLICATIONS FOLLOWING HIS LONG ILLNESS. HIS BODY
WAS PLACED IN A CASKET IN THE GREAT HALL OF THE PEOPLE
AND OVER 300,000 PEOPLE FILED PAST."

Jonathan Spence, The Search for Modern China

CHAPTER 13

A DREAM REALIZED

Lyn and I rejoiced to have the nucleus of a small church meeting in our home, but what were thirty people among Kwun Tong's thousands? When we gazed out the living room window of our fourth floor apartment, we could see the homes of more than 100,000 people, mostly unreached.

As Lyn and I analyzed the situation, we realized one of our key failures. Although we had tried very hard to do so from the beginning of our work, we had not been able to involve a Chinese man in the leadership of the church. We determined to try every method at our disposal to train young men and women for leadership. We began a series of extension classes from HKBBI. If our students did not qualify to go to the school (because many were not high school graduates), we would bring the Bible institute to them.

Using the hour from seven to eight on Sunday evening, just before the evening service, we taught courses for thirteen weeks, with an examination at the end. We taught Bible doctrines and New Testament Survey. We prepared courses in hermeneutics and Bible study methods, and invited other teachers to help our young ladies open a Sunday school for children. At the same time, I tried to give a concrete example of how to study a particular Bible book by preaching through Philippians and Ephesians for thirteen weeks each in the evening service. We also met with all the Christians on Saturday nights, using a Navigators' Bible study course, which made the young people dig for themselves.

The effectiveness of the Commons' Kwai Shing church-planting project and my studies at Portland had convinced Lyn and me that we needed to shift gears even further in Kwun Tong. We had come to believe that a center was the best way to reach the satellite cities, a God-given method that was suited to developing a strong indigenous church in the shortest possible time. Did we have the courage to admit that we had made some mistakes and to make a radical shift in our work at this late date?

Lyn and I began searching for a place where we could open a center in the Kwun Tong area. If we could only find the right site, we could open a center and provide a home for the growing church. But the housing estates in our area were more than ten years old, and the British government had long since allocated all the spaces available for centers.

Sometimes it seemed as if our entire ministry in Hong Kong consisted of looking for space, for apartments, for housing, for parking. Hong Kong's culture was driven by the simple lack of space. However, I discovered that the government, in its perpetual drive to create more housing, was building the new Shun Lee Estate about two miles away, on the other side of a low mountain from Kwun Tong. I set up an interview with the Social Welfare Department.

The chief officer of the department said, "If you're interested in the Kwun Tong area, why go to Shun Lee Estate?" She told me space was available for a center in the Wo Lok Estate, just across the street from our home. Wo Lok was in the center of a huge area with one of the greatest population densities in

Hong Kong. Within just one mile—a ten-minute walk from our home—were four estates housing over 200,000 people.

Lyn and I walked through the estate. Wo Lok Estate housed 12,000 people in ten concrete buildings, some as high as eighteen stories. Bamboo poles protruded from every building, with the day's wash flapping in the wind. The Chinese name of the estate literally means "Peace and Happiness Village." But there was no church of any kind in the estate, and we wondered how many people had real peace and happiness.

Walking northeast toward the valley below, we descended a long flight of stairs and entered the older Kwun Tong Estate, row after row of twenty-four identical seven-story concrete buildings. There were 52,000 people packed into this small area. Each family had a single ten- by twelve-foot room. The estate was a mighty clutter of human activity and noise. We walked through hawkers peddling their wares, children playing their Chinese version of hopscotch, and street sweepers at their endless task. Women haggled in high voices over vegetables and meat. Fish lay on tables, split in half by huge cleavers, their hearts still beating.

Across the road, concrete steps led up the long hillside to yet a third housing estate, Sau Mau Ping. Stacked in this estate were thirty-seven buildings, each fifteen stories high. More than 129,000 people lived on the rocky hillside. Such a population density was nearly unfathomable to us as Americans, but opening a center here became Lyn's and my new dream.

After rejecting applications for a social service center and a youth center, government officers told us that we might be allowed to open a study center in Wo Lok. In May 1977, we sent in the formal application papers and applied for space in a quieter building called Sun On House. While waiting for approval, we needed to gather the resources—both human and monetary—to start the center. I estimated it would cost $12,000 to renovate and equip the premises, and an additional $400 a month to run the center. Our Hong Kong team didn't have those funds, but we asked supporting churches to pray that God would clearly open this door and help us solve all the problems that loomed ahead, or that He would just as clearly close the door.

By differing paths, God brought new workers to the Kwun Tong team. Carol Bibighaus, from Haddon Heights, New Jersey, was an ABWE missionary just finishing language study. While she studied Cantonese, she attended the Kwun Tong church, playing the piano and teaching an English class. When she finished formal language study, she came to work in Kwun Tong full time. The field council approved her new assignment, and Carol helped raise funds for the new center.

Macky Wong was the first Chinese believer to become a vital part of the Wo Lok Study Center team. Macky had been one of the first Christians in Kwun Tong, the first fruits of my class at David College. Her witness had shone brightly, and she had brought many friends to the Sunday evening services. In the summer of 1976, she visited relatives in Canada, but after she had been there for several months, they began to press her to stay. Macky now had to make a decision to stay in Canada, as thousands of Hong Kong young people were desperate to do, or to return home. Canada offered the prospect of a new life, and escape from the perpetual crowding of Hong Kong and the shadow of communism extending across the border from China.

Macky wrestled with her decision until November 1, 1976, when she wrote us, "Last night I made a very great decision in the missionary conference in the Peoples' Church of Montreal. I decided to go back to Hong Kong as a missionary." She returned to Hong Kong early in 1977 and enrolled in HKBBI. Eventually, she came to work in the new study center in Wo Lok.

God continued to bring all the pieces of the project together. During 1977, supporters gave over $23,000 towards the center, and on March 8, 1978, we received the letter we had been waiting for from the Hong Kong government: "I am pleased to inform you that approval has been given by the Hong Kong

Enriching lives
by connecting people
with the power of
words and images.

How can you help?

Classic Arts Programs

Levels of Support

wagon wheel theatre

2006

Damn Yankees
June 7-17

Rodgers & Hammerstein Musical, TBA
June 21 - July 1

Seussical, The Musical
July 5 - 15

Recent Broadway Musical
July 19 - 29

Steel Magnolias
August 2 - 12

Leader of the Pack
August 16 - 25

Second Sunday Series

presented by the Christian Performing Artists' Fellowship and Grace College

Oct. 9- featuring the Warsaw Symphony Orchestra

Nov. 13- The Spiritual Lives of the Great Composers

Dec. 11- our annual Christmas Show

Jan. 8- featuring MasterWorks guest artist John Kasica, principal percussionist, St. Louis Symphony

Feb. 12- our annual Valentine's Day Show

Mar. 12- "Trio Night"

Apr. 9- featuring MasterWorks guest artist Rich Swingle, actor

May 14- Around the World in Music

time- 7:30pm   admission- free   (574) 267-5973

place- Rodeheaver Auditorium, Winona Lake, IN

Housing Authority for allocation of the following. . . ." Months of negotiations had been successful. Fifteen months after we expressed our dreams to the field council, we were able to open a study center in Wo Lok.

Our joy over the building was tempered by our concern for Susanna Chan. Back in 1975, Lyn's mother, Anne Alexander, had met Susanna riding on a double-decker bus. She was returning from a doctor's visit where she had just learned that she had a blood disease. The doctor thought Susanna, who was still in her teens, had only six months to live. "Grammy" Alexander invited her to come to our Sunday evening service. Impressed by Grammy's sincere concern, Susanna came, and she continued to return almost every week. She swiftly became part of the group, loved by many friends for her joyful spirit and perpetual smile.

But her terminal illness hung over her. During one of her many hospital stays, Susanna told Carol Bibighaus, "It's leukemia, and the person who was in the bed next to mine died of it." For a fleeting moment, fear flooded her eyes before her smile returned.

The Christians in our nucleus church drew together as they prayed for Susanna week after week. Though we had discussed Christ with her on several occasions, we were not sure of her spiritual condition. At Sunday night services, however, she always requested the same song, "I know where I'm goin'." We weren't sure Susanna really did.

She was a courageous battler against leukemia. But by the fall of 1977 she was losing the fight. Her hair had fallen out, and her hands and ankles were so scarred from perpetual injections that doctors struggled to find a vein that would still hold a needle. Susanna showed fear of the death that she knew was approaching. Carol Bibighaus, Macky Wong, Lyn, and I took turns visiting Susanna in the hospital, trying to bring peace and comfort. Some days, though, when we saw her pain and suffering, we were reduced to standing by the bed in tears, unable to speak. One particular weekend in the spring, Susanna lapsed into unconsciousness, and we all thought the end was near.

Somehow, though, she rallied, and within days amazed us all by being able to leave the hospital. She came to the services again for several more months. On Christmas Eve, we held a candle-light service and asked those who were following Jesus to light a candle and give a testimony. This time, Susanna gave a clear testimony that Christ was helping her and meeting every need. Hoping to study at HKBBI, she had written her testimony of the great changes God had brought in her life:

> I am sure to say that I have got the greatest treasure that can be found in this world since Jesus Christ accepted me as one of His children. It's really a miracle that after He came into my life, I started to enjoy a new life, with new hope, calm, and peace in my heart that I had never felt before. He gave me strength and bravery, especially when I was in the hospital. He gave me strength and love to challenge the sickness whenever I felt hopeless and depressed. From now on, I am looking forward to living an eternal life with Christ in His kingdom of heaven.

On Sunday night, May 14, 1978, we held our last evening service in the Ambacher home on Yuet Wah Street. After the sermon, carrying hymnbooks and Bibles, we left in a group and walked across the street to the new Wo Lok center where we gathered for the closing hymn and prayer.

The next week, Bill Commons and I flew to Manila to speak at a conference of one hundred ABWE missionaries serving throughout the Philippines. On Monday evening, May 22, Lyn phoned and told me that Susanna had gone to be with the Lord. I went on a solitary walk, contemplating God's grace, demonstrated so vividly in Susanna's life.

At the funeral the following Sunday, the believers from the Kwun Tong church stood and sang the hauntingly beautiful song by John Peterson that had been Susanna's favorite:

> I know where I'm goin' and who I'm gonna see
> I have a friend named Jesus waiting there for me!
> He has given something that only He could give
> He gave his life in payment so that I could live.[1]

On July 1, 1978, Wo Lok Study Center opened its doors to receive students. Two weeks later, we had an official ribbon-cutting ceremony on Saturday, followed by the dedication of the Wo Lok Baptist Church on Sunday afternoon. Friends from all the ABWE churches in Hong Kong joined us to celebrate and thank God. In answer to the prayers of many people, God helped us realize our dream. He gave us the means to plant ourselves in at least one satellite city.

In 1976, after Mao Tse-tung's death, many people dreamed that China would emerge into new life, though it was still too early to predict what direction the country would take. In Kwun Tong, we too had dreamed, only of a new church site, not a country. By 1978, our church had come to life, spurred not by the death of a tyrannical leader, but of Susanna Chan, beloved friend and believer. Susanna's death had united the Kwun Tong Christians in prayer and given us all a greater determination to reach our satellite city for Christ.

"In 1978, the Communist Party Central Committee overwhelmingly endorsed Deng Xiaoping's reformist policies. The external effects of China's political climate were felt first in Hong Kong."

Robert Cottrell, The End of Hong Kong

CHAPTER 14

INTO THE DRAGON EMPIRE

While we were making plans to see the dream of our new church fulfilled, a smaller, personal dream also came true. One morning in January 1978, as I leafed through the morning newspaper, I suddenly came alive with excitement. It was hard to believe the article on the front page. After almost thirty years of prohibiting Americans and most other foreigners from entering China, the Communist government had decided to allow limited numbers of foreigners to enter China on short tours.

Lyn and I had tried for five years to take a trip into mainland China, but were always rebuffed with the excuse that "China does not have adequate hotels and facilities to accommodate tourists." China had been a closed country. The Communists did not want outsiders to see the grim reality behind the curtain, nor did they want outsiders, especially Americans, to stir up dissension amongst the Chinese people. The Great Wall, as has often been remarked, both kept the barbarians out and kept the people in.

With the death of Mao, Deng Xiaoping slowly introduced reforms. The Chinese government took stock of the dire economic situation and realized that tourism could bring badly needed money into the country. China announced that it would work towards a "normalization" of relations with the United States and the world.[1] Not only would the Chinese government profit from eager tourists who would pay anything to get a glimpse into the long-closed country, they would be able to present a sanitized version of China to the world—the new China, the friendlier China—keeping the tourists strictly away from any sight of the excesses of communism.

Within a few hours of reading the article, I rushed to the China Travel Service in Kowloon to complete tour applications. The clerk explained that China would no longer automatically reject our application simply because we were Americans. However, he could not guarantee we would be accepted until the morning the tour left Hong Kong. Four days before the tour departed, we would attend a briefing and hand over our passports. The travel service would take our passports to the Hong Kong-China border, where Chinese visas would be stamped into them. If any applicants were rejected, they would not be informed until they came to the train station for departure on Saturday morning.

When I explained the situation to the family, Lyn was skeptical that our applications would be accepted. We promised each other not to be too disappointed if our applications were turned down. But Kristi, Lori, and Brent were as excited as I was, and we could hardly bear to wait the four days.

At the China Travel Service briefing, I was told to report to the Kowloon Central Train Station on Saturday. Early on Saturday morning, we took a taxi to the train station. At the station, when our passports were handed back, complete with Chinese visas, the children and I could not resist jumping up and down in glee. The only restriction was a prohibition on taking pictures of military installations.

The train took an hour to wind through Hong Kong's New Territories to the border. Arriving at Lo Wu, the town beside the border, we passed through the British checkpoint first. As we walked across the old wooden bridge over the Shum Chun River that marked the actual border, we realized we were the first

ABWE people to enter China in the twenty-seven years since the Barnetts had fled for their lives.

Passing through Chinese customs, we entered the Shum Chun train station and boarded the express train for Canton. Writing tables were placed at each seat, as if inviting us to take notes of this historic occasion. We were too busy looking out the window at the passing countryside to write down our impressions. For years, we had lived in the shadow of the dragon, and yet the mainland had always been an abstract—we had known it was there, worked with its refugees, yet we could scarcely imagine it. Now, China was finally a tangible place. In less than two hours we covered the ninety miles to Canton.

Canton, called Kwangchow by the Chinese, is the largest city in southern China, with over two million people. As we walked out of the station to waiting buses, a large crowd surprised us. We wondered what had brought them out on a dreary, chilly Saturday afternoon. Then we realized they had come to see Canton's biggest attraction of the week—us, the foreigners. Just as the West had vilified the Communists, so had the Chinese government vilified Westerners. If China had only been a shadow country, a country of the imagination, until we finally set foot on Chinese soil, we too must have seemed only specters to the Chinese until they set eyes on us

At every step of our journey, we were accompanied by "minders." Our guides escorted us to the Dongfang Hotel, a new, relatively modern building with large but simple rooms. After a brief rest, we started on an orientation tour of the city, with our first stop the Canton Museum. Seventy-five people were on the tour, divided into three groups, with each group riding on a small, fairly comfortable bus. A guide, wearing a blue Mao jacket and baggy pants, rode on each bus.

As we rode through the city, we were struck by the drabness and absence of color. It was winter, and the atmosphere was cold and subdued. The people wore dark trousers and somber expressions. The buildings were flat and dull, undistinguished by color or human activity. The houses were unpainted, the walls bare, except for occasional propaganda posters. There were almost no cars in the city, and just a few buses, but there were thousands of black bicycles. We saw no cats or dogs in the city, and only a few in the countryside.

The museum was mainly devoted to the official party version of China's history. I was surprised to find pictures of Robert Morrison, the first Protestant missionary to China. Here, Christianity literally had been put into a museum. The captions beneath Morrison's picture explained that Westerners—and particularly missionaries—had been imperialists who took advantage of the Chinese people and forced them "to eat the foreign religion." Lyn and I were the only ones on the tour who could speak and read Chinese. As I explained the signs to some of the English-speakers in our group, the guide walked over, upset that I was translating the captions for the tourists.

"Those things happened a long time ago," he said to me. "Now, we all want to be friends. Anyway, it's time for you to go back to the bus."

He seemed sincere—no doubt he had been warned to control what the tourists saw, but he did want to be friends. However, the Chinese had not had a chance to interact with foreigners for a generation, so honesty and friendship came awkwardly. After supper, we visited a cultural park popular for family outings. On the way, we were struck by the lack of light in the city. Homes and streets were dimly lit, usually with a single low-wattage bulb in the main room. The economy of electricity was a sharp contrast to Hong Kong's unembarrassed extravagance of lights.

The next morning we were led to the Friendship Store, a department store for foreigners. When the Chinese had said in the past that they didn't have adequate hotels and stores to accommodate Americans, they had meant it. These buildings had been constructed in the 1950s for the Soviets. Instead of going to the Friendship Store, I quietly escaped our minders and walked to a local department store nearby. I wanted to see what life was like behind the façade. When I asked the simple question, "Can I buy a hat?" a jostling crowd surrounded me. They were surprised and excited to see a foreigner who could speak Cantonese. Younger people, who had never known life except under communism, seemed afraid to talk with us, and some were even hostile. But older citizens and people in the country areas seemed friendly.

Later that morning, we were allowed to walk down to the Pearl River on our own. Beside the river, Lyn and I felt surrounded by history, walking past places where Morrison and many other missionaries had lived and worked. Our family grew quiet as we contemplated again the significance of our presence in China. We wondered if we would ever again be able to walk as freely as Morrison had.

The Canton Zoo, Asia's largest, was a less serious place. Most of the tourists headed straight for the famous giant pandas, but Lyn and I were more interested in talking with local people. A group of soldiers proved rather unfriendly, but Lyn delighted some housewives and children by talking with them.

"Why do I understand her talk?" wondered a wrinkled old lady as she looked at Lyn. "I can't understand the other foreigners." She paused, and the light suddenly dawned. "Oh, I know why," she said. "She's talking our talk!"

That afternoon we drove to Fushan City, twenty-five miles to the southwest. The group was taken on an extensive tour of a ceramics factory, but after speaking with several workmen, Lyn and I wandered outside. We began to talk with some children, and soon a friendly crowd of over 100 people surrounded us, peppering us with questions.

"Which city is brighter," they asked us, "Hong Kong or Canton?" We were puzzled to know how to explain Hong

Kong's millions of lights to villagers who had never seen anything comparable. Some of the people who lived just across the street surprised us by inviting us into their homes. We wished there had been enough time to accept their offer.

The next cold, raw day we journeyed to a commune twenty miles north of Canton. Walking through the commune's primitive, poorly equipped hospital, we were sobered by what we saw. A Belgian engineer among the tourists, who had spent half his life working in the developing countries of Asia, said that most of the equipment was from the 1930s. The hospital was the worst he had ever seen. Seeing the spartan life on the commune—home to 68,000 poverty-stricken villagers—we thought of our many friends who had fled to Hong Kong, most at great risk to their lives. Even though we knew our guides were allowing us to see only a fraction of real life in China, we understood better why the refugees were so desperate to flee.

In the commune, the twenty-five tourists divided into two smaller groups and entered several homes to talk with the people, who seemed very amiable and accommodating. But because we could understand Cantonese, Lyn and I discovered that the guides told the tourists what they wanted them to hear, whether or not it was factual.

Our group included several Japanese tourists. As we sat down in one home, the housewife began to speak very animatedly in Cantonese. "The Japanese came here in World War II," she said, her voice growing progressively louder. "In our village, the Japanese devils raped, looted, and killed!"

"She says that conditions in this village were difficult during World War II," translated the guide. "But life has been better since Liberation." "Liberation" was the term used by the Communists to refer to Mao's takeover of China in 1949.

As we left the house, I dropped behind the group to talk to the husband. "How long have you lived in this house?" I asked. He looked to be sure no one was listening and then he smiled.

"Oh, I don't live here," he said. "We just use this house to show to groups coming to visit."

On the way back to our hotel in Canton, we passed through a village where we stopped on a narrow street behind two trucks. Hearing noise ahead, our guide climbed out to investigate. He came back to tell us that we would have to wait until the trucks were unloaded. What I could hear sounded like a different story, people across the street were shouting in Chinese: "Fight! Fight! The drivers are fighting."

That night, we were taken to Canton's best restaurant, the North Garden, for a farewell feast. Dish after dish was brought, including some foods we had never tasted before. Many of the Japanese tourists succumbed ungracefully to *mai tai,* the fiery Chinese rice wine. We wondered what the waiters thought, seeing so much food lavished on foreigners, while the diet of their own families was meager and limited.

On Tuesday morning, we made our way to the train station for the return trip to Hong Kong. Waiting in the station, I thought of China's 900 million people. Our guide, Mr. Taam, insisted that no one in China believed in religion, which the Communists called superstition. The fact that our guide had obviously been misled made us realize how much the Chinese people needed God's Truth to sweep away the lies binding them. I stood on the station platform waiting for the train, singing Isaac Watts' majestic song:

> Jesus shall reign where'er the sun
> Does his successive journeys run;
> His kingdom spread from shore to shore
> Till moons shall wax and wane no more.

Our visit to the Dragon Empire had been only a small event, yet it gave us hope that China would someday open. I prayed the day would come when HKBBI students would be able to travel inside China with the message of the Gospel.

DEMOCRACY WALL, BEIJING, CHINA, APRIL 1, 1979

"JUST AFTER THE ANNOUNCEMENT OF ANOTHER GREAT CRACKDOWN,
A YOUNG CHINESE MAN PUSHED THROUGH THE ONLOOKERS AT
DEMOCRACY WALL AND POSTED ONE FINAL POEM, NOW FORBIDDEN,
ON THE ONCE CROWDED WALL, BEFORE SWIFTLY WALKING AWAY
WITHOUT SAYING A WORD."

Jonathan Spence, The Search for Modern China

CHAPTER 15

A CHURCH IS BORN

The year that China first permitted foreign visits, Deng Xiaoping criticized the Maoist political purges of the past decades, proclaiming, "Everyone here is scared—the youth, even more the elderly. That is precisely why our technology is so far behind."[1] Would China's new interest in economic growth put an end to fear and slowly introduce democratic reforms? In 1978, Chinese intellectuals began criticizing the horrors of the Cultural Revolution. In Canton, a group calling themselves the Democracy Movement posted manifestos and poetry on a stretch of city wall, Democracy Wall. In 1979, however, Deng Xiaoping turned against the protestors, and the government cracked down on the fledgling democratic movement.

Returning from our trip to China, Lyn and I wrestled with the knowledge of how privileged we were. Though giving up the "roomy old house and yard in Ohio" for an apartment in densely populated Hong Kong initially felt like a sacrifice, our life was luxurious in comparison to that of the mainland Chinese, perhaps most so because we could proclaim our love of God without inhibition or fear.

In a 1975 article in *Moody Monthly,* Lyn described other women's assumptions about the kind of homes they required: "We need a place to live: a large place, preferably a bedroom for each child where creativity can develop; as far as possible from dirt and noise and crime, a pleasant view, privacy essential."

Lyn's response to these assumptions was to pray: "Lord, here is my sister, a widow with more children than I have. She lives with her family in a dingy room, ten feet square, assembling plastic flowers to scrape together enough money to feed her children and give them a meager education."

The wider missionary community often brushed aside such concerns, saying, "It's all right. The Chinese don't expect us to lower our standard of living. They are accustomed to tiny, crowded rooms, long hours of work, and simple food. They know we could not survive like they do."

As Lyn wrote, North Americans attempted to rationalize their desire for possessions:

> We say we "need" our shag rugs and color TVs, extra cars and air-conditioned comfort, our carefully restored antiques, our campers and our boats. Lord, surely you weren't serious about not laying up treasures on earth, about setting affections on things above, not on things below. That bit in Acts about "having all things common, distributing to each as they had need"— isn't that what the Communists tried on the mainland? Surely we need nice homes to impress our neighbors so we can reach them with the good news. Who would listen to us if we sold our lovely things and began to share with hungry people? We're used to comfort, Lord.

Lyn concluded her article with the image of Christ's sacrifice and servanthood: "He left heaven's glories, took on Himself the form of a servant." God was continually working in her heart, transforming her discomfort into a profound compassion for the Chinese. Our trip to China, where we had seen people's lives made dismal by poverty and repression, only reinforced our realization that we should be grateful not only for God's material blessings, but for the freedom He had granted us. We were called to be servants, to use that freedom of expression to take the Gospel to the Chinese.

*   *   *

In July 1978, we immersed ourselves in preparations for the new Wo Lok Study Center. Christians from our church distributed announcements to every home in the Wo Lok Estate. These brochures invited high school and college-age students to apply for membership in the new center. July was not the best month to open a study center. With schools closed, few students felt the need to study, or to join a center that provided a quiet refuge in the crowded Wo Lok Estate. But it gave us time to work together as a staff and plan for the coming year.

To interest new friends in the Gospel, we planned a week of classes in music, English conversation, and an English book, discussing *In the Presence of Mine Enemies,* Howard Rutledge's autobiography about faith in Christ during the Vietnam War.[2] In spite of a fierce typhoon, which poured twenty inches of rain on the city in two days, fifty young people attended the classes each evening. Coping with Hong Kong's bad weather had become almost commonplace by now.

On July 23, 1978, came one of those disasters missionaries dread but the Lord uses for good. We invited a guest speaker for the evening service but he failed to arrive. With no preparation at all, I spoke from John 6. Though I worried about mispronouncing the Chinese tones, the Lord helped me. At the end of the sermon, I was led to ask those who wanted to name Christ as their Savior to stand up in front of the group. Four young people stood, and after several months of studying in a new members' class, the four were baptized into the church in September.

We set up a program to help the new believers learn to feed

themselves from God's Word. We translated chapters of Tim LaHaye's book *How to Study the Bible for Yourself*.[3] These chapters provided a "Daily Spiritual Diary" which urged the Christians to look for several things in their daily Bible reading: a promise from God, a command to keep, a timeless principle, and an application to life.

The new believers not only profited themselves, they began to reach out to others. Macky Wong had brought Ng Suk-ming to the Sunday evening services several years before. Suk-ming studied quietly and carefully for a long time before she was ready to profess Christ and be baptized in 1976. Now she began to meet each week with a girl named Candy, who was not yet a Christian, quietly discipling her step by step. It was several months before Candy gave public testimony of her faith in Christ, but Suk-ming's patient work paid off.

In the midst of the rewards of that summer, I experienced one of the hardest days of my missionary life. On August 18, Lyn took Kristi to the United States to enter Trinity College. Unlike other parents of college-age children, we knew we wouldn't be able to see her at Thanksgiving, Christmas, or Easter vacations. She wouldn't be able to pop home for a weekend or share a happy moment with us in a quick, cheap phone call. She would be across a vast ocean, on another continent, nearly unreachable for years. I could barely imagine not being able to speak with my daughter every day, as I had her whole life. And I worried that her sudden immersion in the foreign culture of the United States would make her transition even lonelier. I promised Kris I would not cry at the airport, but as hard as I tried, I was unable to keep my promise.

* * *

Then, God gave Lyn, Carol, Macky, and me the last vital member of our Wo Lok team. Teddy Cheng accepted the church's unanimous invitation to become the student pastor of Wo Lok Baptist Church. Teddy was short, barely five feet tall. His high school classmates had called him "The Runt."

As a teenager, to show that he was tough and disprove his nickname, he took up smoking, drinking, and gambling. One Sunday evening, April 7, 1974, Teddy was ambling down a street in Kowloon when one of the Christians from Sunshine Baptist invited him upstairs to an evangelistic meeting in the second-floor apartment. Teddy turned away but the stranger persisted, "You've got nothing else to do, come on up." Teddy reluctantly followed.

For the first time in his life, he heard a clear presentation of the Gospel. In the Fremonts' home, Carson led Teddy to Christ. He was baptized and joined Sunshine Baptist Church in June 1974. He began studying the Bible eagerly in Darline Fremont's Sunday school class and attended every church service.

In 1974, Bob and Sandy Hedrick, from West Virginia, were leading the work at Sunshine Baptist. Bob took Teddy under his wing, training him in almost every phase of church work. When Bob and the other leaders at Sunshine realized God had given Teddy Cheng leadership qualities, they encouraged him to attend HKBBI. In June 1975, Bill Commons urged Teddy to consider preparing for full-time service.

One afternoon Teddy knocked on my office door at the Bible institute. I had already heard the story of his recent salvation. Since we had only seven churches in Hong Kong, each new believer was a special delight to be shared by all the churches. Teddy stood fearfully in my office, worried his high school record was not good enough to qualify for entrance to our school. "Pastor Hon," he said, addressing me by my Cantonese name, "I beg you for a chance to study!" We agreed to let him attend as a part-time student on probation for one semester. If he did well, he could continue with the three-year course.

Teddy not only did well; he was soon a full-time student at

the top of his class. In addition to working hard at Sunshine Baptist, Teddy spent afternoons at the Kwai Shing Christian Social Service Center, presenting the Gospel to the hundreds who came to the center each week. Bill Commons soon promoted Teddy to center supervisor.

Teddy Cheng served at the Kwai Shing center for several years until Wo Lok Baptist Church called him as pastor. He took over the student pastorate at Wo Lok with enthusiasm. Young people responded quickly to his leadership. By October, more than fifty students came to the study center each day. Every week, Teddy led the Wo Lok Christians in personal evangelism classes and special prayer meetings for a Sunday night evangelistic meeting to be held in January 1979. The Christians divided into two groups and distributed invitations to the service to over 5,000 homes in the Wo Lok and Kwun Tong estates.

In the late fall, Teddy and I steadily prepared for the January service. Then, one rainy morning, I woke up with pain in my side so intense I fainted. Lyn rushed me the six miles to Evangel Hospital, but in the gridlock that Hong Kong calls traffic, it took over an hour to get there while I rolled on the back seat and floor of the car. The problem proved to be a kidney stone too high to pass. In November I ended up in Baptist Hospital with a seven-inch incision in my side and an expensive stone in a bottle. I was laid up for weeks. Through the Lord's providence, Pastor Teddy and the Wo Lok believers *had* to take over all the organization for the January evangelistic meeting.

Teddy invited Pastor Steve Trinh, Calvary Baptist Church's second Chinese senior pastor, to be the speaker for the meeting. Pastor Trinh was a gifted evangelist from Vietnam. Calvary Baptist had experienced a growth spurt under his dynamic leadership. By 1977 the church had over 100 members, and no more chairs could be squeezed into the auditorium.

In October 1977, after paying off the loan on three apartments, Calvary became ABWE's first church in Hong Kong to start a daughter church. Choosing a crowded housing estate called Pak Tin about a mile away from their own building, members from Calvary began an evening service. They were able to borrow a clinic's facility for the purpose. In 1980, Calvary would open an elderly center in Pak Tin to make more contacts and provide a home for the new church. Many people were responsible for the rapid growth at Calvary, but it was obvious that Pastor Steve Trinh's leadership was the key factor—our hope that Chinese leadership would transform our church plants was already being realized.

When Pastor Trinh spoke at our January 1979 evangelistic meeting at Wo Lok, he employed skillful humor to captivate the audience, then convince them of the urgency of his message. Eight people made public professions of faith in Christ and went into adjoining rooms to talk with counselors prepared in Teddy's classes. Lyn and I were grateful that Pastor Trinh was such a good model for Teddy, and we prayed that Teddy would also become an effective leader in the Wo Lok church plant.

On May 20, 1979, Teddy Cheng completed his studies at HKBBI with the highest academic average in the history of the school up until then. That same afternoon he announced his engagement to Jennifer Tse, one of the first Christians in the Kwai Shing Baptist Church. Jennifer was well prepared to serve beside Teddy—they had already studied together at HKBBI and worked together in the Kwai Shing Center. She, too, was tiny, only four feet eleven.

On May 27, while Pastor Teddy led the service, I baptized five more young people into our Wo Lok Baptist Church. The congregation was full of joy as Stanley Mak prayed for the first time and Tommy Yiu gave his first testimony: "I praise God; He has given me salvation and made me so happy."

The following week, Teddy Cheng became Wo Lok's first full-time pastor. When Lyn and I left for our third furlough on May 30, 1979, the church was independent in all but name. The

Wo Lok believers were governing their own church, they were supporting it, and they were definitely evangelizing their own area.

Our principles had been taken and put to work. Teddy and Macky had not only been taught at the Bible institute, they were being steered at the new Wo Lok Baptist Center and Church, putting into practice what they had learned. All our work of the last decade had led up to this moment. To have a part in the birth of Wo Lok was one of the greatest experiences of our lives.

1980–1987

YEARS OF GROWTH

DECEMBER, 1980, BEIJING, CHINA

"MAO'S WIDOW, JIANG QING, ON TRIAL WITH THE GANG OF FOUR FOR
'PERSECUTING TO DEATH 34,800 PEOPLE AND HAVING FRAMED AND
PERSECUTED 729,511 OTHERS,' WAS DRAGGED SCREAMING FROM
THE COURTROOM, DEFIANTLY SHOUTING AT WITNESSES AND
CALLING THE JUDGES 'FASCISTS AND GUOMINDANG.'
SHE WAS CONDEMNED TO DEATH."

Jonathan Spence, The Search for Modern China

CHAPTER 16

THE 1980 MIRACLE

Lyn, Brent, and I spent the furlough of 1979–1980 in
Rockford, Illinois, since Kristi and Lori were both studying in
the Chicago area. Kristi was studying sociology at Trinity College
and Lori was majoring in creative writing at Wheaton College.
Lyn and I always loved to return to the United States for furlough, to experience the wonderful changes of season—cool
spring, resplendent autumn, so refreshing after the relentless
humidity of Hong Kong—and to reunite with family and
friends. But our children had spent almost all their lives in Hong
Kong, and the United States was not home to them. Despite
Brent's skills as a rugby player, the other students at West High
School found it hard to believe that he was not familiar with
American football and baseball.

During furlough, we prayed for months about whether or
not to remain in the States while our children were in college.
Today, ABWE and other mission agencies offer transition programs to help missionary kids—or Third Culture Kids, as they

are sometimes dubbed—adapt to life in the United States after they return from the field. Just as missionaries receive language training and learn about their adopted cultures before they leave for the field, missionary kids now receive "language and culture" training for life in the United States. However, in 1979, transition stress was not yet widely recognized, and though we knew our children were struggling to adapt, there was not much of a support system for them, and no MK Relations department to track their progress. After much prayer, we felt our work in the Bible institute was not complete, nor was our work in church planting. In retrospect, I often wish Lyn and I could have stayed with our daughters for part of their college years. But in 1980, Lyn and I returned to Hong Kong.

This term would be different, for many things had changed. Brent returned to King George V School, but he was lonely with both big sisters gone. He worked with his good friend Rob Paswaters, cleaning the Heritage Kindergarten every weekend. At the field council's request, Lyn and I agreed to move into one of the apartments ABWE had purchased in Mei Foo, the middle-class housing development where Bob and Margaret Paswaters had started Heritage Baptist Church.

In our absence, Wo Lok Baptist Church had seen amazing growth under Teddy's leadership. We had left a nucleus of about thirty people, and now seventy-two attended the morning service. Lyn and I had considered not returning to the church after furlough. We felt we should give Teddy the freedom he needed as a new leader. Mei Foo was far enough from Wo Lok to provide the distance between us and the church.

Then, our first Sunday back, I assisted Pastor Teddy Cheng in baptizing seven new graduates of a baptismal class. He urged me to stay and work with him. He saw the need for mature Christians at Wo Lok, since so many there were new young Christians. "Pastor Hon, we need at least a few 'white heads' around here," Teddy cajoled. We agreed, but Lyn and I resolved to be extremely careful not to overshadow Teddy and his new wife, Jennifer.

* * *

With Teddy Cheng in charge of the church, we were able to give more attention to the Bible college. When I assumed the leadership of Hong Kong Baptist Bible Institute in 1975, our HKBBI Committee had spent much time discussing the needs of the school and developing a ten-year plan. In the last five years, we had begun to implement the plan: working to recruit students, improving the course selection, and involving both teachers and students in church planting—Teddy and Jennifer were prime examples. We had also hired our first Chinese teacher, Lawrence Loo, who had earned his master's from Dallas Theological Seminary after graduating from HKBBI. Dallas was the first U.S. seminary to accept one of our graduates.

As a result of our changes at HKBBI, we had seen our enrollment gradually grow, but the third stage of the plan, finding a new location and creating a larger dormitory, was still to be achieved. While we searched for property, real estate prices skyrocketed. Missionaries were paying up to $700 a month to rent a small flat. Citibank predicted the rental rate would soon rise to $1,000 a month.

Then, Far Eastern Broadcasting Company (FEBC) suddenly announced it was moving from the two flats adjacent to HKBBI. The company offered to sell us the 4,200 square-foot property for 20 percent less than the open market price. It was an unprecedented opportunity, but we simply didn't have the funds to meet the price: $650,000. Wendell Kempton had become ABWE's third president in 1971. He was a visionary, with a great heart for people. By 1980, Dr. Kempton became convinced that we had to take strong action if the Hong Kong ministry was to grow significantly. When he heard of FEBC's offer, Dr. Kempton printed this challenge in the Fall 1979 issue of the *Message,* ABWE's official magazine:

> The Hong Kong field council faces an unprecedented challenge. What we do about it right now will determine our future in the evangelization of Hong Kong and China. We must move now to purchase missionary housing. We face an even greater problem with our present Bible institute. We desperately need room to expand our program into a full-fledged Bible college. We must have $650,000 to pay for the school property and housing by December 31, 1979.[1]

Dr. Kempton and those missionaries who were on furlough traveled around the United States presenting the challenge. In a few months, just enough time to purchase the property, over $700,000 was given to the "Hong Kong-China Emergency Fund" from over 4,000 different donors—more than we had even requested. We called it the "Miracle of 1980," a description which seemed appropriate to the whole decade of the 1980s, when missions in Hong Kong would suddenly ignite.

During the next months, HKBBI's governing committee took advantage of FEBC's offer. In 1979, we had owned one apartment on the second floor of a twelve-story building. Now we had purchased the two adjacent apartments, almost quadrupling our previous usable area. The three-year course finally became a full-fledged four-year Bible college program, with a Bachelor of Christian Studies degree and two majors: Theology and Christian Education. We changed the institute's name to China Baptist Theological College (CBTC). Through God's good timing, I had just finished my doctorate at Western Seminary, writing my project on church planting in the satellite cities. I was hopeful that my Doctor of Ministries degree might bolster CBTC's reputation in Hong Kong.

Before CBTC could open, interior renovations were needed.

One morning I was in my office asking a government official whether we could be exempted from paying property taxes when Carson Fremont shouted from one of the classrooms: "Rats! Twelve of them in one cage! A world record!"

Lyn wrote home a half-gleeful, half-horrified account of the rat invasion at the "famous" China Baptist Theological College: "Recently we have had quite an influx, but unfortunately, not of students. RATS—big and little, old, young, and pregnant. We have had half the government's pest control department in here. One poor female got caught in a trap and proceeded to produce eleven offspring. The false ceilings and recessed light fixtures make an absolutely perfect home for Mum and all her 'rittens.' Yesterday one particularly happy fellow chewed through the wires in the ceiling of my office and sparks shot up."

Fortunately, we were able to control the vermin. As the new college prepared to open, the Lord supplied personnel to teach the students we hoped would come. Susanne Farley had arrived from Nebraska in 1976. Now, she slowly developed the Christian Education Department, gathered materials in both English and Chinese, and demonstrated their use to students. Later, Sue would serve as an invaluable assistant to the president. She was a skilled listener to the students, something that was especially needed because most of them came from non-Christian homes. Sue is still on the field, and holds the record as the longest-serving ABWE single woman missionary in Hong Kong.

Norm and Louise Barnard, from Michigan, were two other arrivals. Norm taught Old Testament courses and became the academic dean of the college in 1982. Like Sue, he developed great rapport with the students, who felt they could always talk with him. He often was seen chatting with students in his office. He was known for his hearty laugh, but I appreciated Norm and Louise even more for their ability to give an honest assessment of every situation, while remaining unruffled.

With more time to concentrate on CBTC, Lyn and I instituted a student retreat that would begin every school year in September, taking place at a camp in the New Territories. Lyn described one of our later retreats in a 1983 prayer letter: "The CBTC Retreat at the High Island Reservoir was a smashing success. Our students are very much city kids and reveled in the lovely outdoors. They loved the archery lessons, basketball, ping-pong, badminton, bicycles, kayaks, and swimming pool. Of course, it would not have been a real Hong Kong camp if the sink had not been totally stopped up."

As God put all the pieces into place, the college continued to grow. We began the new four-year course in September 1981 with six full-time students. We set a goal of recruiting at least four new freshmen each fall and a total student body of sixteen. We believed that we needed at least four graduates each year for the growing ministry in the colony. China Baptist Theological College was gaining respect in the city, as demonstrated at CBTC's Sixteenth Annual Bible Conference in March 1982. Dr. Philemon Choi (Brent's pediatrician) spoke on "Problems in the Family." More than 1,000 people attended each night of the conference, held in a church rented for the occasion.

By the summer of 1982, we had three Chinese teachers. Another important sign of growth came when the local Chinese churches began to support the college. In the school year just ended, 31 percent of the college's annual budget of $25,000 came from Hong Kong churches. The evening school program regularly had sixty or more students. As students became excited by their evening school study, some gave up their jobs and entered the full-time day program at the college. We were thankful for the vision of Dr. Kempton and the ABWE administration. They had helped us turn the corner in our efforts to build a "major league" college.

Though Lyn and I missed the daughters we had left behind, God provided us with great joy, as we saw the institute transformed into a college and our church plant thriving under Teddy

Cheng's leadership. The "Miracle of 1980" would not only inspire us in our next term, it would set the pattern for God's extraordinary work in the next decade.

HONG KONG, 1980

CHAPTER 17

JEWELS IN THE CROWN COLONY

By 1898, the British Empire had not only acquired Hong Kong Island and Kowloon permanently, but had signed an agreement with China leasing the New Territories for ninety-nine years. Part of Hong Kong was borrowed land, living on borrowed time, and in 1997 the lease would expire. In 1980, the British government began to make secret attempts to address the problem of the lease. In Hong Kong, the business community was growing increasingly nervous as the prospect of Communist rule drew nearer. Fearful of angering the Chinese with a direct proposition, the current governor of Hong Kong, Murray MacLehose, made a quiet visit to Deng Xiaoping, suggesting that if China allowed Hong Kong to issue commercial leases beyond 1997, investors would have faith in the future of the colony. But Deng replied that Hong Kong was part of China and indicated his desire to recover the colony according to the new "one country, two systems" policy. MacLehose's attempts at negotiations were rebuffed, although the British government would continue to interact with the Chinese government in the next decade.[1]

However, MacLehose did not return to Hong Kong and report the news. Instead, he repeated Deng's official request that the investors in Hong Kong set their hearts at ease. Instead of reading between the lines, many people in Hong Kong accepted this statement as evidence that China would allow Hong Kong to remain under British rule past 1997.[2] Hong Kong was useful to Mao as an independent colony, so they reasoned the Communists would still need them now—functioning as a full capitalist society.

At the same time, the Communists mounted an intensive campaign to transform their image and bring new investors and companies to Shanghai. Business boomed, and the property market in Hong Kong accelerated.[3] Many people in Hong Kong were blinded by prosperity. The colony became a consumer's paradise. Tourists flocked to avail themselves of a treasure trove of electronics and jewels. But the citizens were more anxious for the future. The fear they felt of the impending takeover would be a great factor in many Chinese turning to Christ.

During the 1980s, we discovered a different set of jewels in Hong Kong: men and women bought by the blood of Christ. Under the leadership of Teddy Cheng and his wife, Jennifer, Wo Lok Baptist Church was bringing many students to Christ. At Sunshine Baptist, Teddy had learned how small fellowship groups could help members grow in their spiritual lives and give them a sense of family. Pastor Teddy introduced similar groups in the Wo Lok church for junior high, high school, and college students, as well as for working people. The principles of internship that we had been trying to implement were valid not only for CBTC, but also in a local church like Wo Lok.

The church burst with activity on Saturdays, and what people remember most was the laughter. Many believers later testified that it was the warmth, the fun, and the fellowship of these

groups that attracted them to learn about Christ. Many people
came to salvation in these fellowships, and some met their mates
there as well. Chinese believers were finding the first real friendships of their lives. On Sunday mornings after the service, hardly
anyone went right home. Young people stayed nearly an hour
afterwards, chatting, catching up on news, and sharing prayer
requests. Newcomers were always welcomed by three or four
smiling young people who seemed honestly interested in them.
After a while, members and visitors filtered out into nearby
restaurants in Kwun Tong, informally, a dozen in one group,
twenty in another.

I was amazed at the wisdom Pastor Teddy showed for a relatively new Christian. One of the few times we disagreed was over
the length of the sermon. I was always careful to keep each sermon to thirty minutes, but he regularly preached for fifty minutes. One day I spoke with him, fearing he would drive people
away if he preached too long. He listened thoughtfully to my
opinion and then responded: "The believers only get one preaching time all week." The small groups that met on Saturday were
largely given to interaction and fellowship with short devotion-
als. "They need one good session for solid Bible study," Teddy
argued, "and thirty minutes is not enough." I concluded that he
was right. Teddy always held the people's attention.

During Christmas in 1980, Wo Lok church was more
crowded than ever. One of the young people who came to the
Lord that Christmas was ten-year-old Mak Chi-fai. He had been
attending Sunday school for about a year. He had believed in
Christ as Savior, and he urged Pastor Teddy to let him be baptized. The churches in Hong Kong did not usually baptize children so young, but Teddy promised to talk with him again and
meet his parents after the busy holiday season.

On January 13, Chi-fai was playing on a concrete playground at school when he fell and hit his head. The harried
emergency room doctor in the local hospital examined him and

sent him home. That night he slipped into a coma, was rushed back to the hospital, and underwent brain surgery. The next day the doctor explained the surgery had been too late, and Chi-fai would certainly die within a week or two. The young people at Wo Lok prayed fervently, but on January 20, 1981, Chi-fai died. I stood in the hall of the hospital and held his father while he wept on my shoulder.

Impressed by the love and concern shown by the Wo Lok believers, the Mak family asked us to hold a Christian funeral service. Land-scarce Hong Kong had only a few funeral parlors, so Chinese and Western funerals used the same parlors. On a weekday afternoon in a small facility on a hill overlooking Kowloon, Pastor Teddy led the memorial service for Chi-fai. As the Wo Lok believers walked back down the hill after the service, Teddy asked me to preach the following Sunday. Many relatives and friends of the Maks attended, and I used the opportunity to speak about heaven.

Afterwards, Lyn and I and the Chengs often visited the Maks' home. Chi-fai's eighteen-year-old brother, Mak Chi-chung, professed faith in Christ and was baptized the following fall. Mr. and Mrs. Mak attended church for awhile, but eventually stopped coming. Many churches in the United States wrote that they were praying for them. We wanted so much for the Mak family—and everyone else who lived in Wo Lok Estate—to know and understand the hope of the Gospel. God would answer our prayers for the Maks, but not for many years.

Through the winter and spring quarters, Lyn taught a Sunday school class for Form 6 and 7 students. Many of them were preparing to take exams that they hoped would allow them to enter one of Hong Kong's three main universities. This was a huge challenge, however, since places were so limited. Less than three percent of Hong Kong's middle school students were able to go to university at that time.[4] The pressure of preparing for exams weighed enormously on the young students. One was

Edwin Fung, whose father scolded him for "wasting" too much time in church. Edwin told Carol Bibighaus, "I think my father loves me. He provides food, clothes, and an education for me. That means he loves me, doesn't it?" Edwin confided to us how hard it was to prepare for his college entrance exams with his family of nine living in a flat of just 300 square feet. Instead, he chose to study at the Wo Lok Study Center, a five-minute walk from his home and school.

At the center, he met Macky Wong, who would have a profound effect on his life:

> It was Macky Wong, the center supervisor, who showed us the love of God in a human form. Her witness, both verbal and non-verbal, made me reflect on the issues of life. Baptized as a Catholic at a very young age, I knew I had sin deep inside, but I had never dealt with it. As I reflected on these problems, I knew only Jesus had the answer to them. Macky and others invited me to the Sunday service and the Saturday fellowship. I was converted in 1979, and the Lord Jesus saved me from my sin.

Edwin joined Lyn's Sunday school class and became part of one of the most intelligent and challenging groups Lyn had ever taught. Edwin was a close friend of four other boys in their late teens, and their testimonies were particular "jewels" for Lyn and me. Jered Kok was the "the tall skinny guy with the big smile," a fine singer, a boy with a probing, insightful mind. He knew Bible verses and hymns, and even prayed at school. But as he said, "I had no life inside me." In 1978, when he was a Form 4 student (high school sophomore), Jered joined a Christian fellowship group at his school: "I was impressed by the Christians' joy, their testimony, and their faith in facing hardships. There was a little voice in my mind that told me something was living inside those Christians."

Jered started to search for a church. He prayed for wisdom, and just after his prayer, members of Wo Lok Baptist gave him a tract inviting him to the study center and church: "After about a year, in 1979, I decided to believe in God, confessed my sins and accepted the Lord Jesus as my Savior. When I made this decision, I felt that I was set free. I had the hope of eternal life and a new life goal in my heart."

Ben Yeung, another member of the class, recalled those life-changing days:

> 1980 was such an important year for me. Being a Form 6 student (high school senior), I had to prepare for the university entrance examination. I needed a place where I could concentrate and master all the lecture notes. I found a small but quiet place near my school—a study center operated by Wo Lok Baptist Church.
>
> As a typical Hong Kong student, I always had an unhappy look as I studied. In fact, it was rare to see a happy face as exams drew near. But in the Wo Lok center, I was attracted by several people who always seemed to be smiling. I could feel the joy and peace in their hearts.
>
> One of my classmates, Timothy Chiu, was invited to Wo Lok Baptist Church, and very soon he told me he had become a Christian. I could see the change in him. He was no longer pessimistic and grumbling. He was filled with hope, he cared about the people around him, and his mind was filled with peace, even in the face of the stressful examinations that were approaching.
>
> My curiosity drove me to see what had changed him. I accepted his invitation and attended a church service at Wo Lok. I found many friendly people, who encouraged and consoled me when I was in despair. I sensed their very real love. I started to read and meditate on the Bible. I began to attend the youth fellowship and the Sunday school, and learned more about God and His love.
>
> After about six months, I knew more about God. I recognized my sin and knew that I could not solve the problem by myself. At an evening evangelistic meeting, I decided to follow Jesus and accept Him as my Savior.

Because it was such a crucial time in their lives, the young men and women took the class very seriously. Lyn later said that it had been the most challenging group she had ever taught. She also found it the most stimulating. "It was as if God had prepared me my whole life for this group of young people at this time," she reflected.

The energetic students raised many questions and entered into vigorous discussions. Lyn tried to be patient in answering even the simplest question. One particularly difficult question was how to reconcile evolution and the Bible—as the students crammed for their exams, they were faced with the need to square the secular curriculum with what they were learning in their Bible studies. Lyn had researched the topic of evolution and creation in great detail in her college days and was, therefore, well prepared to interact with the students.

As the months went by, Lyn was able to lead some students to the Lord. Pastor Teddy prayed with others, and Macky Wong was also a testimony. The whole team was thrilled when all five young men were admitted into university. Edwin began to study medicine, and even his father was impressed. Maybe church was not such a waste of time after all!

Hong Kong had always been the jewel in Britain's imperial crown, but for Lyn and me, and surely for Teddy and Jennifer, the new Chinese believers—Jered, Edwin, and many other students—were far more precious. They were jewels in the crown of Christ, not the crown of the Lion Empire, and nothing, not even the shadow of the seemingly amiable Dragon Empire, could diminish their brilliance.

LONDON, 1982

"The People's Liberation Army could overrun Hong Kong
at any time, and Britain could do nothing about it."

Sir Percy Cradock, Foreign Affairs Adviser to Prime Minister John Major

CHAPTER 18

GRACE PROVIDED

In 1981, Lyn noted the arrival of the new governor of Hong
Kong, Sir Edward Youde, an "old China hand" from the British
Foreign Department: "Youde is considered something of a China
expert, knows Mandarin, but not Cantonese. I suspect the need
for negotiations with China over what happens in 1997 influenced the decision to choose Youde. We rather hate to see good
old Governor MacLehose go." Lyn and I still did not know the
degree to which Hong Kong's fate as a colony hung in jeopardy.
We were concerned more with the incredible workings of God's
grace throughout that year, in every aspect of our lives and ministry, than with the future of Hong Kong.

As Lyn and I worked together with Teddy and Jennifer
Cheng, our lives became more and more intertwined. Jennifer,
like Lyn, was particularly good with the students at Wo Lok, and
she counseled many of the teenaged girls. She was keenly sensitive to the difficulties new believers faced as they struggled to live
as Christians in Hong Kong, negotiating the demands of family
and work. Like Lyn, she also had a keen mind, and had completed several years at Bible college. Her hunger for knowledge
and her skills in counseling made her an ideal helper for Teddy.
We rejoiced to see the young couple working as a team, and I
was reminded again of how integral Lyn was to my own work—

she provided the heart of all our interactions with believers.

On April 3, 1981, Lyn and I were delighted when Teddy and Jennifer's daughter, Grace, was born. Her Chinese name, Ying-yan, meant "special love and grace." But she weighed less than five pounds at birth and developed jaundice soon after. The doctor warned that if she did not begin digesting food soon, she could die. The whole church held special meetings, praying that she would recover. Finally, fourteen days later, Grace was able to digest a little food, and soon came home from the hospital. The next Sunday morning, after the service, Pastor Teddy came up and laid her in my arms. I held her, and through my tears led the church in a prayer of thanksgiving. Grace would become like a granddaughter to Lyn and me. Over the next weeks, Lyn enjoyed helping Jennifer with her new baby.

Wo Lok Baptist Church continued to grow at an extraordinary rate. By the spring of 1981, Sunday morning attendance was averaging eighty people. One Sunday in June, 126 attended, and at another service we had twelve new professions of faith in the same morning. Teddy and I realized the study center auditorium would soon be unable to accommodate more people. It was time to think about planting a daughter church. In 1981, Lyn and I began to consider where we could start a second church.

Teddy and I knew that the study center method had proved to be a fast and effective way of developing an independent church. Our ABWE missionaries and Chinese pastors wanted to open more study centers. Though the number of ABWE church plants had grown, nine churches seemed only a handful in a city with a population exceeding five million.[1]

As ever, our church-planting efforts would be influenced by the housing policies of the Hong Kong government. Housing was a perennial struggle. In August 1979, caught up in an inter-departmental debate, the Hong Kong government had stopped granting sites for study centers in the housing estates. The Housing Authority did not want to open further study centers, believing their job was to provide housing, not places for study. The Education Department fought with equal vigor for places in every housing estate where students could study quietly.

Hoping to learn whether sites might be granted in the future, I went to ask a friend at the Housing Department, Mr. Yao (not his real name). I knew that if I could see him, I could learn the government's current stance. But Mr. Yao was an important man in a high position, and his vigilant secretary guarded his office door like a sentinel. As I took the elevator, I prayed that God would help me be able to see him. When I peered down the hall, I could see his watchful secretary seated at her desk.

Suddenly, Mr Yao walked briskly up behind me and put his arm on my shoulder. "Mr. Ambacher, are you coming to see me? Come right in, come right in," he repeated.

After polite greetings, I came straight to the point. "Mr. Yao, our agency urgently needs at least two new sites for study centers, and I have come to urge the government to change its policy and begin to allocate study centers again."

"Who leaked my report to you?" he interrupted. "How did you see my report?"

"I don't know what report you're talking about," I protested.

His expression softened. "The government has just changed its policy. A study center will be allocated in any housing estate that does not currently have study places. We will work first with applications that we have already received." He indicated a sheaf of papers on his desk. "These letters on my desk are going out in the next few days to agencies all over the city, inviting them to apply for study centers."

He explained that after fulfilling this initial lot of thirty-six study centers, the government would only allot a few centers in the future. He suggested that we could amend our application to include more sites. If I could return it immediately, our amended application would be given priority.

"I can't tell you the names of the thirty-six estates where

centers will definitely be granted in the future," he said, pointing to a list on his desk. "But I have to leave my office for a minute. If you happened to look at this list while I was gone, I couldn't prevent you, could I?" He left the room.

Half-stunned, I stared at the list, trying to memorize the page before rushing away to write down the names.

The next weeks passed in a whirlwind of visits to the housing estates on Mr. Yao's list. ABWE missionary men and pastors, including Norm Barnard, Pastor Teddy, Yeung Po-wan, Po-wan's deacons, and Bill Reid, took turns accompanying me. We regularly prayed the prayer of Nehemiah each time we visited a government official: "O Lord, I pray, please let your ear be attentive to the prayer of Your servant, and to the prayer of Your servants who desire to fear Your name; and let Your servant prosper this day, I pray, and grant him mercy in the sight of this man" (Nehemiah 1:11).

We spent hours discussing possible new sites with all the ABWE missionaries and Chinese pastors. Our missionary force had shrunk from twenty-five to ten people. Some had retired, some had been assigned to administrative positions in the ABWE office, and others felt they didn't fit in Hong Kong. Because of our reduced numbers, we might not be able to handle multiple sites. Yet this seemed a unique opportunity. Mr. Yao had, through God's grace, given our field council the greatest advantage it ever had.

Rushing against time before the sites would be allocated to other groups such as the Buddhists, the ABWE field council came to a consensus we believed was directed by the Holy Spirit. Our field council unanimously agreed to apply to the government for six new sites for study centers and churches. We formed teams of one missionary and one Chinese pastor for each of the sites we might receive.

Pastor Teddy and I were assigned to start a study center in the Shun On Estate, just one mile from Wo Lok, if that site were granted to us. One sunny afternoon Teddy and I visited Shun On, discovering to our delight that the estate's bays were longer than usual. We estimated that a church service of 140 people could fit into one bay.

"Pastor Hon," Teddy exclaimed, "this site is the most ideal of all the locations we have visited." The two of us stood beneath the huge thirty-story building and prayed that God would allow us to start a church there for His glory.

Applying for six new sites was a bold step for our field council. We had never applied for more than one site at a time before, and we had never started more than two churches in one year. I wrote to the presidents of three colleges in the United States: Dr. Mark Jackson at Baptist Bible College of Pennsylvania, Dr. Paul Dixon at Cedarville College in Ohio, and Dr. Wilbert Welch at Grand Rapids Baptist College. I urged each of these friends to ask their students to pray that our application might be successful:

> We desperately need to get at least two sites to start new churches in 1982. What a wonderful thing it would be if you would be willing to enlist your student body to pray for this one simple request. We don't need money. But we do need God's people to lay hold on Him so that He will turn the hearts of the government officials involved in making these key decisions.

Conscious that ABWE was not the only group of God's people working in Hong Kong, I wanted other mission agencies to share in God's grace. I phoned Jack Campbell, the chairman of the Christian and Missionary Alliance (C&MA), and met him for lunch. I explained the government's new position and urged Jack to submit an application as soon as possible. With this new information, C&MA updated their application and eventually received several new sites. I also phoned Dick Baucum of Baptist Mid-Missions (BMM) to pass along the news of a possible site in Butterfly Bay. Dick and I visited the man in charge of deciding who would get the site. He made a verbal promise to award the site to Dick, and within a year BMM opened a church there.

As far as our own applications, we had done all that we could to seize the opportunity opened through God's grace. Now we could only pray and wait to see if our applications would be approved.

* * *

While we waited, Lyn received another chance to enter the Dragon Kingdom when a new friend, Ruth Borofsky, asked Lyn to accompany her to Beijing. Ruth had been on a tour to Hong Kong and China with a group of people from Philadelphia when she fell on the plane coming to Hong Kong and injured her leg. While she recovered, the tour group had left without her.

Lyn was reluctant to leave Brent and me, but we argued that we would be fine. "Go!" we urged her. "If we had the chance, we would go." Ruth and Lyn flew into Beijing in the bitter cold. Wrapped in Chinese "great coats," they walked on the Great Wall with an icy, biting wind howling around them. Lyn was frustrated that no one understood her "southern dialect" of Cantonese in the far north of China, where Mandarin is spoken. Though everyone in China was supposed to be equal under the Communist system, Lyn easily spotted party leaders who were "more equal" than others. Their uniforms were made of much finer material.

On a cold, shining day, Lyn visited the "Temple of Heaven." The lofty, round temple with its twelve massive pillars, had been erected for the god of heaven whom the earliest Chinese people had worshiped. It was an ancient place, monumental in its beauty, but it was not the dwelling place of a god. The heaven it imagined was desolate, inhabited only by the wind. Lyn stood in the temple and cried out to the one true God for the people of China.

Lyn returned from her trip sobered by the Chinese people's

great need for God's grace, but exhilarated by the experience of having visited China once more. We were all the more eager to see study centers open in Hong Kong, waiting impatiently for the response from the government to arrive. But then events intruded into our personal lives and consumed all our thoughts. Kristi and Lori were due to graduate from college one year apart. Brent's grueling examination schedule prevented Lyn and me from attending the graduations together. Instead, we decided I would attend Kristi's graduation in May 1982, and Lyn would attend Lori's in 1983.

Then, in March 1982, my father learned he had Hodgkin's disease. After forty days in the hospital, Dad seemed to be improving. I had already bought plane tickets for the planned trip for Kristi's graduation. So rather than changing my flight to visit him immediately, I proceeded with my original plan. I left Hong Kong on May 11, 1982, and flew to Chicago to spend time with both Kristi and Lori. I phoned Dad from Kristi's; he talked briefly and sounded well.

But the day before I arrived in New Jersey, he grew faint and slipped into unconsciousness. My older brother, Richard, rushed him back to the hospital in an ambulance. When I went to his room, Dad was unable to recognize me. I visited him in the hospital every day, and a week later we were all relieved when the doctors said he was gaining strength again. His sudden death on June 7 came as a complete shock.

My return flight to Hong Kong was scheduled for that very day, for my brothers and I had never expected the funeral to be so soon. I would gladly have paid $800 to change the ticket, if only I could have had the chance to talk with Dad again, but he was gone. My brothers agreed that it had been far more important for me to visit Dad while he was still living than to attend a service after his death. So, numbed to the core, I embarked on the plane mere hours after Dad's death and flew back to Hong Kong.

I was too heartbroken to talk. Each query of the stewardess

fell on me blankly. I sat in the stiff airplane seat, consumed by my grief, feeling profoundly alone. The flight to Hong Kong seemed as if it would be unbearably long. But when I changed planes in Chicago, I saw an old friend, Paul Tassell, the national representative for the General Association of Regular Baptist Churches. His daughter, Jill, was flying with a group of students from Baptist Bible College on a summer trip to the Philippines. Jill had been assigned by the computer to sit next to me on the flight to Tokyo, and the other BBC students were in front of me, behind me, and on my other side. It was as if God had assigned them to accompany me on the long flight across the Pacific.

* * *

When I arrived back in Hong Kong, Lyn and I felt overwhelmed by the great distances that separated us from our family. We had never been so frustrated that our service for the Lord required us to be so far from home. In the weeks that followed Dad's death, Lyn and I often walked in the evening by the ocean near our apartment, our hearts aching.

During my short time in the United States, I had preached in a large supporting church. The deacons had urged me to allow the church to vote on my name as their potential pastor. Still grieving, I wondered if this was the Lord speaking, and if it was time to return to the United States. Now, in Hong Kong, Lyn and I asked the Lord to show His will clearly. After several weeks, I wrote a letter to the church deacons, telling them to proceed. I signed the letter, sealed it, and left it on my desk. Lyn and I agreed that unless the Lord showed us otherwise, we would mail the letter in two weeks.

Then on June 26, I came home for lunch and found the long-awaited answer from the Hong Kong government's director of housing. I tore the letter open expectantly, to learn that the government was initially granting us one study center and church site, in the Shun On Estate in Eastern Kowloon near Kwun Tong. I remembered Pastor Teddy exclaiming that this was the best of all the sites, and I pictured him and me standing in that bay, praying for God to give us the Shun On site. I knew this was God's answer to our prayer for His leading, and I tore up the letter to the church in the United States.

In the months to come, God continued to answer our prayer for more church-planting sites. First, Heritage Baptist was granted a site on Tsing Yi Island and started a daughter church there in 1982. Heritage's Pastor Yeung and the deacons had been inspired to action as they helped us search for sites.

When I visited a government office a few months later, Mr. Nigel Ma, of the Social Welfare Department, pressed me, "Let's talk about present possibilities rather than future ones. Why don't you take the elderly center site that is available *now* in the Lai King Estate in Kowloon?" I phoned Norm Barnard and Leo Lam, one of the six church-planting teams we had formed. Together with Leo, the pastor of Kwai Hing Baptist Church, Norm opened a church and elderly center in Lai King in 1984.

Another application for the Tai Hing site in the distant New Territories satellite city of Tuen Mun, previously named Castle Peak, had been unsuccessful on the first try. Bob and Margaret Paswaters applied to the Housing Authority again, and this time the site was awarded to them. The Tai Hing Baptist Church and Study Center opened in 1984.

In a stupendous answer to prayer, God had given us four new sites for center-churches in response to our specific requests. It had taken eighteen years for ABWE to open our first four churches in Hong Kong, and eight years more to open the next four. Now we had opened four churches in just fifteen months.

Profoundly thankful and conscious of being present at an historic moment for ABWE, Lyn and I sent an "Emergency Praise Letter" to our supporting churches and college students telling them the results of their prayer campaign. When the students at

Cedarville College heard our letter, they broke out in applause. God had heard His people and answered dramatically. Lyn and I had much to look forward to in the coming years as we worked together with Teddy and Jennifer to plant the new church at Shun On.

The Satellite City
of Junk Bay

Grace and Joyce Cheng, 1984

ABWEs second president,
Dr. Harold Commons, surveying
Junk Bay with Harry, 1987

View from our 24th floor apartment
on Ferry Street, 1986

Lyn with the keys to the newly opened church and center in Po Lam Estate, Junk Bay, 1988

.Harry and Teddy at Po Lam Baptist Church dedication

Construction of Garden Estate, 1990

Brent with ABWE's third president, Dr. Wendell Kempton, in Kowloon, 1989

Children at the Garden Estate Baptist Church nursery

Teddy, Jennifer, Lyn, and Harry at Garden Estate dedication, 1991

CBTC students on the Mount of Olives overlooking Jerusalem, 1991

Harry teaching CBTC students in front of the bema (Judgment Seat) in Corinth, 1993

CBTC students at the Acropolis in Athens, 1993

CBTC graduating class, 1994

Harry and Lyn riding into Petra, Jordan, with CBTC students, 1996

Lyn, sick but still smiling, with grandchildren Anne and Walter, Rockford, Illinois, 1998

BEIJING, CHINA, SEPTEMBER 1982

"I DIDN'T REALIZE THAT THE CHINESE WOULD OVERTURN
A TREATY WHICH GAVE US SOVEREIGNTY OVER HONG KONG.
BECAUSE IF YOU DO THAT, YOU'VE NO INTERNATIONAL LAW
AND NO TREATY IS EVER WORTH ANYTHING."

—*Prime Minister Margaret Thatcher*

Robert Cottrell, The End of Hong Kong

CHAPTER 19

A DAUGHTER CHURCH
AND A GRANDDAUGHTER

On July 4, 1982, Wo Lok Baptist members rode one mile on
the red, double-decker 26M bus, chugging slowly up a steep, picturesque hill to the Shun On Estate, where we inspected the site
the government had awarded us in On Chung House. North
Americans may wonder why we would start another church just
one mile away from Wo Lok, but within that one-mile radius lived
200,000 people. Shun On Baptist would be the only church in
an estate where over 13,000 people crammed into four buildings.

I traveled five miles to the site almost every afternoon after I
finished teaching at CBTC. Thankfully, I could ride the new
Mass Transit Railway (MTR) most of the way. Our lives were
greatly simplified when the first branch of the MTR opened.
The MTR was a world-class feat of engineering, equaling the
Metro in Paris and the Underground in London. The transit
authority proudly claimed that trains ran at two-minute intervals
during rush hour. For the first time, we could speed under traffic
jams on the air-conditioned MTR, and it was no longer neces-

sary to drive to many parts of Hong Kong. This change brought more benefit to our lives than any other single factor in many years. In fact, this was the first term in Hong Kong that we felt it was not necessary to have a car, and without the need to drive in Hong Kong traffic, our tension levels dwindled.

The Shun On Center opened on November 8. Within a few weeks, sixty students were using the center every day. Every bill was already paid when we opened. Since the United States was in a recession, we had not wanted to appeal to American churches for funds. Instead, we asked the Lord to bring in the needed amount without our making any public announcement. The initial amount of $12,500 came from funds Bill and Sharon Commons had raised to start several new study centers and churches. A leading Hong Kong bank awarded us a grant of $12,000. The Wo Lok church gave $4,000, and other special gifts came in without our saying a word. The Lord's provision had been swift and comprehensive.

In September 1982, while we were renovating the center, England's Prime Minister, Margaret Thatcher, flew to Beijing to begin negotiations with the Chinese. According to the three treaties signed between Britain and China in 1842, 1860, and 1898, Hong Kong Island and Kowloon had been ceded to Britain permanently, while the New Territories had only been leased to them for ninety-nine years, to be returned to China on July 1, 1997. Since Hong Kong had become one of the most prosperous cities in the world, with a gross national product greater than most countries, the British hoped that China would extend the lease for at least another fifty years.

But the Communist government of China believed it had been humiliated by the "unequal treaties" with Britain and was determined to regain its "lost territories." Very early in the negotiations with Prime Minister Thatcher, the Chinese shocked the British by informing them that they would not extend the lease by even fifty days. Furthermore, they announced that they intended to recover not only the New Territories, but also Kowloon and Hong Kong Island.

As negotiations dragged on for the next two years, the British realized two important facts. First, if they were to give the New Territories back to China, it would not be feasible to govern Kowloon and Hong Kong Island by themselves. Most of the new housing, the airport, and half the new subway line were in the New Territories. In addition, most of the colony's water was piped from China through the New Territories. Kowloon and Hong Kong Island could not exist without the New Territories.

Second, the British realized that while they had only a few thousand soldiers on the land mass of Asia, China had a standing army of 4.2 million, the world's largest, with the ability to put millions more in uniform, if necessary. The British negotiators' backs were against the wall. Although Thatcher tried to take her typically firm stance with the Chinese, she made very little progress.

In Hong Kong, people were finally beginning to realize the implications of the negotiations, and the currents of fear grew stronger in the colony. Regardless of the result of the negotiations, we knew that we were in Hong Kong to pursue God's work, and that if Hong Kong was truly running out of time, it was all the more important to plant as many churches and reach as many people as we could before the Communists resumed rule. In 1982, the year 1997 still seemed distant, but we knew it was drawing ever closer.

In December 1982, we held several Christmas evangelistic meetings in Shun On, while Wo Lok's members prayed about who might volunteer to go as "missionaries" to help start the new church. At the dedication service for Shun On in January 1983, Wo Lok Baptist Church also announced its independence. I was to remain only as an advisor to help with government matters. My work would continue at CBTC and with the Shun On plant. We began evening services in Shun On on April 3, with twenty attending. Committed to the growth of Shun On, Wo Lok sent seven members to join the church-planting team, and the Wo Lok young people distributed literature to over 4,000 homes in the Shun On Estate.

God sent special people to work on the Shun On team, including Elijah Wong. Many Hong Kong young people take an English name when they begin school, and some Christians later change their English name to a Bible name when they receive the Lord. Thus, Nelson Wong called himself Elijah. Elijah had been a schoolteacher when he became a Christian. Although he believed the Lord was leading him to study in CBTC, Elijah postponed his study for several years until he had saved enough money to provide for his widowed mother. Then he gave her the money and explained that God was calling him to prepare for Christian service.

Elijah not only volunteered to help us start the Shun On church, he also took the job of supervisor of the study center. I rode the MTR and then a bus to the new center several times a week to meet with him. Elijah sat at the desk near the entrance. We charged less than $1 for a six-month membership, as a way of preventing troublemakers. But students were so glad for a quiet, air-conditioned place to study that we never had to expel any students. Most of them were in middle school or college, and Elijah made friends with many of them.

The housing manager of Shun On proved to be another friend, not just a government official. He warned us that the estate was a difficult area because so many residents were such recent immigrants from China. Among these newcomers were Mr. and Mrs. Choy. They attended the first church service in the new Shun On Baptist Church. When they returned late in April, they unburdened their hearts to Lyn and me.

Once again, as Lyn and I made ourselves available to the Chinese, we were unexpectedly drawn into their lives. The Choy's only child, Jack, just thirteen, was involved in a gang that had gotten into a fight over a girl at school. Seven boys had taken a schoolmate into the lavatory and beaten him to death with a wooden stool.

Although Jack swore he was not the killer, if the gang were found guilty, he would share responsibility under Hong Kong law. The government decided to try Jack and three of his schoolmates, ranging in age from thirteen to seventeen, for murder. The Choys were ignorant of Hong Kong law, and I helped them sort through the red tape and find out how to get free legal representation. I spent many hours in court with Mrs. Choy, trying to comfort and advise her. Mr. Choy claimed to be a Christian, but showed very little understanding. Mrs. Choy made no such claims, but seemed more interested in learning. Lyn and I hoped that they would grow in their desire to learn about Christ.

Then, in the summer of 1982, while we were trying to help the Choys, a massive rainstorm hit Hong Kong. Twenty-five people died in landslides and floods. Over sixteen inches fell in one twenty-four-hour period. It continued raining for three days. Roads were flooded, schools closed, and all water restrictions removed. Hillsides collapsed, and mud and cement covered the cities. More than twenty ships ran aground. Ten people died; thousands were left homeless. *The South China Morning Post* reported that "tons" of chickens and pigs drowned, and vegetables were washed away. Market prices nearly doubled. In the streets, people said that the typhoon had caused Hong Kong's "golden fortune" to run aground.

Since our apartment was just one block from the South China Sea, we were directly hit by the storm. Within a few hours, we were without elevators, electricity, gas, drinking water, and flushing water for the toilets. At its highest, the flood waters flowed waist deep on our street. It was a full week before everything was restored. I had to hoist buckets of water from a fire hydrant on the street up to the eighth floor, all the while holding a candle or flashlight to see on the pitch-black stairs.

Lyn described the aftermath of the storm in a letter to Kristi and Lori: "This morning as I waded through mud and water to get to the MTR station, I passed several dozen women cheerfully washing their clothes under running water from the fire hydrant. Several people in their pajamas were washing up, brushing their teeth, and spitting beside the shiny marble wall of the Hang Seng Bank."

The typhoon was the worst we had ever encountered in Hong Kong, and Lyn and I were thankful for the protection God had granted us and the Wo Lok and Shun On believers. As Christians, their greatest concern was to help others. In the churches, it was common to take secret love offerings to pay for the funeral of a church member or someone in his family, because most people in Hong Kong did not have life insurance. As a whole, people in Hong Kong tended to react stoically to natural disasters. By the end of the summer, the city had returned to normal.

In November 1983, I traveled to the High Court in Hong Kong Island's Central District to attend Jack Choy's trial. The Hong Kong trial was frustrating, because the British laws put the Chinese at such a disadvantage, even though the Chinese made up 98 percent of the colony's population. The judge was English, wearing an English robe and wig. Jury members and witnesses were required to speak English—which none of the Chinese defendants understood. I spent many hours translating for the families. Several times the judge rebuked me for talking to the families in court. On December 2, the case was sent to the jury.

While the panel of seven was deliberating, I talked with the Chinese police sergeant who had prosecuted the case.

"If you win a guilty verdict, will you feel some satisfaction?" I asked him.

"Not really," he answered. "It just means I will go back to my desk and deal with the rest of the cases that are stacked up there."

He was honest in admitting his life was not very satisfying.

"My younger brother told me I should become a Christian," he said.

"You should listen to him," I answered, but just then our conversation was interrupted by the cry, "The jury is coming back."

They had been out for six hours. Now the verdict was announced—in English—and the mothers of the boys looked at me in desperation. I translated the verdicts for them: the jury acquitted one boy, found one guilty of murder, and two others—including Jack—guilty of manslaughter. How do you gently tell a mother that her son, who had just turned fourteen, has been convicted? On December 16, Jack was sentenced to a minimum of six months and a maximum of three years in a training center for boys.

Jack had displayed an appalling lack of remorse, admitting to me that he had used a wooden stool to beat his schoolmate to death. They had been rivals for the same girl. He insisted the dead boy "deserved it." While we could not dispute the conviction, Lyn and I were deeply saddened by the pain it caused the Choys, and by Jack's utter hardness of heart. Though we did not know if the Lord would ever soften any of their hearts, we could only pray that the time we had spent with them would plant a seed that might some day grow into faith.

Less sobering than our involvement in the lives of the Choys was Lyn's and my continued work with Pastor Teddy and Jennifer Cheng, who were mature and wise beyond their years. Their daughter, Grace, was now two. As a tiny girl, she had started calling me "A Yee," which means "Second Aunt." We didn't know why she chose this name rather than "uncle" or "grandfather." Her parents were on a campaign to train her to be more polite, and told her that she must call me "Hon Muk Si," or Reverend Ambacher. Wanting to be good "grandparents," we tried not to interfere when her parents urged her to obey.

One day at the Bible college, Grace came running towards

us. She was trying to comply with her parents' instructions, but became confused. Turning to Lyn, Grace called her "Reverend Ambacher," called me "Second Aunt," then fled away as fast as her little legs could carry her. On October 17, 1982, the Chengs had a second baby girl, Pui-yan, which means "More Grace." In English, they called her Joyce.

While Lyn and I taught at CBTC and worked at the Shun On church and center, Brent completed what would be his last year in the Hong Kong school system. One crisp fall afternoon he helped King George V School's rugby team defeat their traditional rival, the Hong Kong International School, 15–12, and was promoted to the first team for his efforts. But he had suffered a slipped disc during the game, and his rugby career ended. Brent's PSAT scores put him in the ninety-ninth percentile of high school students in the United States, so we realized he also excelled off the field. As we prayed and talked with Brent about his further education, he applied to the Stony Brook School on Long Island for his senior year of high school and received a scholarship. In 1984, he graduated from "The Brook" with honors.

In March 1984, when the steering committee from Wo Lok Baptist Church shifted services in Shun On to Sunday morning, the attendance increased to thirty people. Once a month, after the morning service, the group at Shun On joined their Wo Lok friends for lunch and the Lord's Table. We all spent time trading news about our respective church-planting efforts. As we neared our summer furlough, we rejoiced that the Shun On church had grown as much in one year as our first church in Wo Lok had grown in eight years.

A few months later, we planned a party in our home for the volunteers who helped at the study centers in Wo Lok and Shun On. These volunteers were high school graduates who took turns sitting at the registration desk for four-hour shifts, saving the centers hundreds of dollars. Lyn was at her happiest when our home was filled with laughing, shouting young people.

"I spent all day Saturday getting ready for the big party," she wrote. "The volunteers came before five and left about ten. They devoured everything I had prepared: ham, chicken, spaghetti, potato salad, fruit salad, and jellos. When I ran out of spaghetti, they put the sauce on bread. Some even mixed potato salad and jello together. They got so hilarious playing games, I thought our glass tabletop might suffer a fracture!"

* * *

The chattering, happy students were in sharp contrast to many of the inhabitants of Hong Kong. By 1984, lack of progress in the negotiations between the Dragon and Lion empires had struck fear in the hearts of many. Half of Hong Kong's people had been born in China; most had fled to Hong Kong to escape from communism. They were afraid to live under the Communists again. Longtime columnist for the *New York Times* Jack Anderson, wrote, "Already billions of dollars have scurried quietly out of Hong Kong, and businessmen are making preparations to relocate." The Hong Kong dollar—one of the world's most stable currencies for thirty years—crashed by 40 percent between late 1982 and late 1984. The stock market slumped 21 percent in a single day and soon dropped to half of the year's high. Property values slumped badly and visa applications to emigrate doubled. One survey showed that 90 percent of Hong Kong's medical doctors planned to leave.

Hong Kong's citizens had no voice or vote. The British governor was appointed by the queen and was a virtual dictator. On April 20, 1984, reports historian Robert Cottrell, "There were gasps in the Legislative Council and many people broke down in tears as British Foreign Secretary Sir Geoffrey Howe announced, 'It would not be realistic to think in terms of an agreement that provides for British administration in Hong Kong after 1997.'"[1]

Without consulting the people of Hong Kong, Prime Minister Thatcher returned to Beijing in December 1984 and signed a treaty agreeing to all the terms demanded by China.

"BRITISH SIGN AWAY HONG KONG— PANIC GROWING IN COLONY!"

The December 1984 headlines screamed from newspapers and magazines all over the world. *The New York Times* reported: "There was no rejoicing in Hong Kong tonight as the governor revealed details of the accord while a dismal rain fell over the city."[2]

The agreement stipulated that Hong Kong Island, Kowloon, and the New Territories would all revert to China on July 1, 1997, but that for fifty years Hong Kong would become a "special administrative region" with a capitalist economy under Deng's formula: "one country, two systems." Though Beijing would control foreign and defense policy, Hong Kong would remain largely autonomous economically, continuing as a free port and world financial center. Rights and freedoms, such as freedom of religion, were allegedly guaranteed for fifty years.[3]

But in 1984, the same Chinese government that promised religious freedom to Hong Kong after 1997 unleashed a new wave of persecution against the Christian church in China. "Hundreds have been arrested, some tortured, in the first sweeping crackdown against the church since 1979," reported *Time* magazine.[4] This was in spite of the fact that the constitution of China "guaranteed" religious freedom. It was understandable that 85 percent of the colony's people did not approve of the new treaty, according to frequent polls taken by the media. The Hong Kong Bar Association voted against support of the agreement, but this gesture was a meaningless token.

Many critics considered the British government to have betrayed the people of Hong Kong. Because they were fearful of provoking outright conflict with China, the British had bowed to the Dragon Empire and failed to secure any real protection of the freedom and rights of Hong Kong citizens.[5]

Yet, as we prepared to leave for furlough in Ohio, Lyn and I were thankful that news from the churches in Hong Kong was anything but pessimistic. One missionary wrote, "This has been one of the greatest periods for growth and fruit that we can remember here." By June 1985, Wo Lok would be averaging close to 140, the capacity of the auditorium, and Shun On had averaged over fifty since March. During our furlough, we would already be considering the question of where and when to start a third church with some urgency.

God had blessed Wo Lok's first daughter church, and as Lyn and I returned to the United States, we received news of yet another birth. Our daughter Kristi, married two years before, gave birth to Anne Elizabeth on March 28. Lyn flew directly to Chicago to see her. At the end of CBTC's semester, I followed her, and finally met "Miss Anne," our adorable granddaughter.

1988–1994

YEARS OF FRUIT

HONG KONG, DECEMBER 1984

"THE CURRENT SOCIAL AND ECONOMIC SYSTEMS IN HONG KONG
WILL REMAIN UNCHANGED, AND SO WILL THE LIFE-STYLE.
RIGHTS AND FREEDOMS, INCLUDING THOSE OF THE PERSON, OF SPEECH,
OF THE PRESS, OF ASSEMBLY, OF ASSOCIATION, OF TRAVEL, OF MOVEMENT,
OF CORRESPONDENCE, OF STRIKE, OF CHOICE OF OCCUPATION,
OF ACADEMIC RESEARCH AND OF RELIGIOUS BELIEF
WILL BE ENSURED BY LAW IN THE
HONG KONG SPECIAL ADMINISTRATIVE REGION."

Treaty between Britain and China, Clause 5

CHAPTER 20

JUNK BAY

During furlough, Lyn began work on a master's degree at Ashland Seminary. She had always had a keen mind, but she wanted to be even better trained to teach—her discussions with her inquisitive Sunday school classes over evolution and other difficult topics made her yearn to learn more. We kidded Lyn when she earned a 3.9 grade point average, out of a possible 4.0. How dare she only get an A– in Old Testament!

When we flew back to Hong Kong on August 18, 1985, Brent stayed in the United States to start college. For the first time, we were alone in Hong Kong, juggling multiple responsibilities as we shuttled between CTBC and Shun On church and oversaw the opening of a third church in Junk Bay.

As ever, we were initially overwhelmed by Hong Kong's extremes: the roar of noise, the crowds, the pungent smells, and the lashing of typhoon rains. We were back in the "land of sweat" as Lyn called it, "the land of warm water coming from the cold water tap; mold on cupboard doors and floors; black, sooty film on floors, shelves, plant leaves, books, and tables; and crowds pushing and shoving everywhere."

We found a small apartment on the twenty-fourth floor of a twenty-nine-story building with stunning views of the harbor. From windows on three sides of the apartment, Lyn watched the endless, tumultuous activity of the neighborhood: "The endless construction and destruction, piles of debris, holes, boards, pipes, baskets, cats, carts, cardboard, slippery slop near the cooked food stalls, stuffed green peppers and bean curd in boiling oil, buckets of viscous dishwater, adorable tots in uniform dragged along by big sisters and brothers, pushcarts, brooms, goods vehicles, drying orange or lemon peels spread out on newspaper, a raw pig on a man's shoulder—and on and on."

Our flat was located at the corner of Ferry and Pitt streets, only one mile from CBTC. For Lyn, Pitt Street opened up new opportunities for ministries of compassion. As she explored the neighborhood, meeting vendors in the market, she discovered that Pitt Street was also the working location for several prostitutes. Setting out to befriend them, she learned one of the women had a daughter who was a nurse in Boston. Lyn also learned that a group of homeless men slept under the Ferry Street flyover (overpass), a block from our new home. She often took soup to them, and when the weather turned cold, she carried blankets and quilts down to them. As always, Lyn was concerned for those who slept in the cold while she was warm in her apartment—even if that apartment was only 384 square feet in total, smaller than most Americans' living rooms. She continued to carry a burden for Hong Kong's poor and dispossessed.

In 1985, dispossession on a grander scale was the subject of constant conversation. British expatriates discussed the impending handover, wondering whether to leave the colony and return to the cold shores of England before 1997 arrived. Most Chinese in Hong Kong had no such choice. The English government had passed laws restricting the immigration of Chinese born in the Hong Kong colony—whatever the conditions were like under the Communists, most Chinese would have to stay.[1]

As the field council chairman, I sent a simple questionnaire to all the missionaries and Chinese pastors, asking what goals we should set to achieve by the 1997 turnover. I was surprised at the near unanimity of the answers. Both groups said that before 1997, they hoped to see the Bible college achieve independence. They also wanted to see ABWE establish twenty-five independent local churches. We had fifteen churches at the time, but only half of them were independent, led by Chinese pastors.

Since both Wo Lok and Shun On churches were close to capacity, Pastor Teddy Cheng urged us to apply before furlough for a third church-planting site—it would fill the need and bring us one church nearer to our goal of twenty-five local churches. So we began the long process of site applications again, the slow courting of bureaucrats which had characterized all our years in Hong Kong. Junk Bay, the eighth and final satellite city, seemed our best option.

Junk Bay had been named for the fishing boats that had sheltered there for centuries. But junks would not be seen on the water again, for the entire bay had been filled with earth, one of the most massive projects the British government of Hong Kong had ever untaken. Located on the extreme eastern end of Kowloon peninsula, five miles from Wo Lok Baptist Church, the satellite city was scheduled for completion in 1986. The Housing Authority planned to house 200,000 people there initially, growing eventually to 380,000. In all our years in Hong Kong, the need for housing would never cease, for the population never stopped growing.

On November 27, 1985, Teddy and I met with government officials. They promised to lease us a site in Junk Bay's Po Lam Estate, if we could submit a careful plan showing we could manage the project. They were particularly concerned that we demonstrate sufficient funding to operate the center. The Po Lam Baptist Church and Elderly Center was tentatively scheduled to open a year later in November 1986.

For two rooms on the ground floor of a thirty-five-story building, the government's official cost estimates for construction costs and furnishings totaled $37,820. Toward these costs, we only had a gift of $7,500.

So in June, I returned to the foundation that helped us fund the Shun On center. Their office was located in Central, the heart of the business district on Hong Kong Island—rather like a larger version of Wall Street. I took the six-minute, one-mile Star Ferry ride across Hong Kong harbor, through a maze of freighters, fishing junks, and yachts. Though the harbor had long since been polluted, it was still spectacularly beautiful. The office I entered was lushly decorated, covered with the thickest carpet I had ever seen. My feet sank into the deep plush as I walked forward.

"What can we do for you today, Mr. Ambacher?" the British banker asked.

"We need a grant of $30,000 for construction of an elderly center in Junk Bay," I began, preparing to offer a detailed explanation of why the need was so urgent.

"That should be no problem," he interrupted. "Is there anything else?"

He shuffled papers on his desk, obviously very busy. The appointment lasted all of two minutes. So much for slow negotiations with bureaucrats—the Lord had provided our entire funds in one swift step.

With the funds ready, I drew up and signed an agreement with the government listing careful plans for the construction of the Po Lam Baptist Church and Elderly Center, now planned to open in 1987.

While construction of the estate proceeded, Lyn and I divided our time, working at CBTC and Shun On, and continuing to prepare for the Junk Bay center. At Shun On, God answered our

prayers by sending Caleb Shum to be the pastor at Shun On
Baptist Church. With a Chinese pastor, Shun On could finally
become independent. Pastor Caleb was a graduate of Alliance
Bible College on Cheung Chau, an island in Hong Kong's New
Territories. He was engaged to Charis Chiang, a Hong Kong girl
he had met while taking further studies in Taiwan. Friendly and
a good preacher, Caleb accepted the church's invitation just
when he was needed most.

* * *

Meanwhile, under Teddy's capable leadership, Wo Lok Baptist
Church continued to grow. Our biggest problem was a happy
one, trying to find more space for people who wanted to attend
the services. Teddy and Jennifer's daughter Grace was in her last
year of a three-year kindergarten program, and Joyce, three years
old, was just starting. Jennifer was busy keeping the family running, while Teddy was studying for his master's degree, supervising the church plant at Shun On, and teaching at CBTC—he
was a hard worker, always managing many tasks at the same time.
Almost every year I would preach a sermon in chapel on the
need for occasional relaxation, using the text, "Come apart and
rest for a while." Inevitably, Teddy would follow a week later with
a sermon on how it is better to "burn out than rust out."

With our own children grown, Lyn and I found our lives
changing. After a long day teaching at the college and supervising one or more of the centers, we exercised several times a week
at the Kowloon Cricket Club. For twenty-three years, I had
made a habit of running three miles a day, three times a week—
it had always been a time to release tensions and to gather my
thoughts. Now, I ran three or four miles along a path beside the
harbor, while Lyn walked around the cricket pitch. We would
have a quiet dinner together and talk over the day's events before
taking the MTR subway or splurging on a taxicab back to the

apartment. We savored our new freedom, but we were always eager for news of our children, and we were proud of their accomplishments.

Lori had received her master's in creative writing from the State University of New York (SUNY) in Binghamton. Kristi lived in Illinois with lovely two-year-old Annie. After a year of college in the United States, Brent returned to Hong Kong to take a semester of Mandarin at the Chinese University.

Lyn often enlisted Brent to help as her "soup and blanket carrier" to the homeless in the neighborhood. He briefly stayed with us in the flat on Ferry Street, while trying several different jobs. He was six feet tall, and his bedroom was so tiny that every night he had to make a choice: he could close his bedroom door, or he could stretch out his legs. He wasn't able to do both. The living room was so small that when Brent sat on the couch, he could put his feet on the opposite wall. But we had spectacular views of Hong Kong Island and Victoria Peak. The sunsets were especially stunning, and Brent would often call us to the living room to see them: "We have to get our money's worth out of this apartment!"

By January 1987, the building in Junk Bay, called Po Tai House, was nearing completion. Glenn and Jean Schumaker, life-long friends and faithful prayer partners from our home church in Ashland, Ohio, came for a visit. Wearing hard hats and walking through the dust, Glenn and I were able to stand for the first time on the site that would become the Po Lam Baptist Church and Elderly Center.

* * *

In early February, Lyn and I were invited to speak at the Bangladesh Field Council's Spiritual Life Conference. For the first time we would see Bangladesh, or East Pakistan as it was formerly known, the country where ABWE had originally assigned us to work. We flew to Chittagong, the main port city of Bangladesh, where we had expected to dock twenty-three years earlier. The country's second largest city was a mass of cows, water buffalo, rickshaws, baby taxis, and men, men, men everywhere, all competing for the same limited road space.

Leaving Chittagong, we rode in a van to Memorial Christian Hospital in Malumghat. It was moving for us to stand beside Harry Goehring's grave there and ponder the perfect, yet sometimes unfathomable, ways of our omniscient and loving heavenly Father. We once thought the Goehrings and the Ambachers would work together translating the Scripture in the land now called Bangladesh. Now one Harry was in heaven, and the other Harry was serving in Hong Kong.

The whole journey was like a visit into a past that might have been. After the conference, ABWE missionary George Collins drove us to Hebron, the jungle station where we had planned to live. After George parked the van, we walked through the jungle for another half-hour, sunlight spilling down in huge golden coins through the glossy leaves.

As we came into the clearing at Hebron beside the Matamahari River—one of the most remote places in the ABWE world—houses built on stilts amid tall green trees rose up before us. I didn't think I could have survived there without my morning newspaper, coffee shop, or subway ride to work. But catching her breath, Lyn exclaimed in awe, "Isn't this the most beautiful place you have ever seen!" We had always known that she would have savored the verdant spaces of East Pakistan, if only we had gone there.

Lyn later described Hebron to her sister: "If we could have survived the day-to-day living (food and shelter), I think I probably would have loved Hebron, a compound set on a hill, with huge trees, wild flowers, and the river below. It was a beautiful place, so quiet and peaceful."

Lyn was happy and satisfied after more than twenty years in

Hong Kong, and confident that the Lord had steered us there in His wisdom. But as I stood looking at her, with her smiling face upturned to the sun, I wondered how our lives might have been different if we had come here, to this quiet place, far from the noisy tumult of Hong Kong. Lyn, too, was thinking of the work we might have done: "We both wondered again about the still unwritten tribal languages."

But God had chosen to send us to Hong Kong. I thought again of the joy of standing beside Teddy, picking out the site for Shun On, or clambering through the dust of the new Po Lam site with my friend Glen, and I knew that God had greatly blessed Lyn and me. Somehow, He would provide for those still untranslated tribal languages. We were already impressed with ABWE's continually growing literature and Bible translation work in Chittagong.

At the airport in Dhaka, the capital of Bangladesh, we had an encounter with the rarest of celebrities—a humble one. As we sat in the departure lounge, talking about our fascinating visit, Mother Teresa walked into the lounge wearing a simple white sari. I was too shy to strike up a conversation with her, but Lyn, always gregarious, was not. These two gentle women were soon sitting side by side, engaged in conversation about their respective heartbeats, which included the poor and homeless. It was as if God had arranged a special farewell to Bangladesh. Lyn admired Mother Teresa and was glad to meet and chat with her.

* * *

We had only been back in Hong Kong a few days when my older brother, Richard, phoned from Philadelphia on February 18 to tell me that our mother had inoperable cancer of the pancreas and perhaps only six months to live. In our twenty-five years with ABWE, it seemed there had never been a more impossible time to leave the field. We were right in the middle of the Junk Bay project, and were both involved in teaching and managing CBTC. But Lyn and I knew we had to go.

At the March field council meeting, our colleagues made one of the most visible demonstrations of teamwork we had ever seen. Bob and Margaret Paswaters, already experienced at constructing several centers, volunteered to steer the Junk Bay project in our absence. Carson Fremont agreed to take over the leadership at CBTC again, and Sue Farley assented to handle CBTC's finances.

On April 23, Richard phoned to say that the cancer in Mother's liver had "gone wild." Fortunately, we were able to get seats on a flight two days later. We arrived in Philadelphia the day after Mother returned from the hospital. We had the privilege of caring for her around the clock, giving the rest of the family a much-needed break. It gave us time to talk with her and to meet her pastor. We were so thankful for the privilege of demonstrating our love, rather than just expressing it verbally. We stayed for seven weeks. After Lyn flew to Chicago to see her parents, I cared for Mother for two more weeks. It was hard to leave, knowing that I would not see her again in this life, and I cried for many miles as I drove to meet Lyn in Chicago. Mother would die on October 6, a month after her seventy-third birthday.

* * *

Lyn and I returned to Hong Kong in July 1987 to a new disappointment—the government had been forced to stop all construction in Junk Bay. "Settling" was expected of buildings in satellite cities built on land reclaimed from the sea. But in Junk Bay, the land was settling more than normal, and everything came to a halt while the engineers tried to discover the reasons.

It was not until fall that engineers solved the problem and the outside shells of all the buildings were completed. All over Junk Bay, roads and sidewalks were being finished, sewers and gas systems were being installed, and schools and markets were being erected. The huge new city was coming alive, like a giant rising to its feet.

As Junk Bay neared completion, the Wo Luk and Shun On churches were blessed with a series of celebrations. In June, Teddy received his master's degree from Hong Kong's Evangel Seminary. On September 25, God gave Teddy and Jennifer Cheng a baby boy named Timothy, or Yan Ho. Then on October 10, Caleb Shum, new pastor of Shun On, married Charis Chiang. This was a difficult wedding sermon for me to preach, knowing my mother's memorial service was being held the same afternoon halfway around the world. Lyn and I knew that Christ had defeated death, and we were thankful that one day He would put an end to all death. But I still felt the sting of grief, even on this day of new joy for Caleb and Charis.

In December 1987, four Chinese pastors and I were invited to form an ordination committee to examine Teddy Cheng. The majority of the dozens of people now attending Wo Lok and Shun On were Teddy's "spiritual children," and most were present for the service. When I led in prayer, asking God to bless *ngoh ge jai*—my son—I couldn't help crying. Lyn and I marveled again that God had allowed us to work with such a special servant of God.

The study centers at Wo Lok and Shun On had been relatively easy to manage, and student study centers had proven to be a remarkably effective method to start churches. But the elderly center at Po Lam was going to be much more complicated. The government required us to hire a full-time staff of four workers. We were also required to have a managing committee. For the next ten years, Teddy and I would spend countless hours in committee meetings—steering the centers we started.

As we looked for "managers," as the Hong Kong government called our committee, the Lord provided three men who had originally been students in Lyn's Sunday school class at Wo Lok

Baptist Church a decade before. Dr. Edwin Fung, the boy whose father had declared church a "waste of time," was now an ear, nose, and throat specialist at the Prince of Wales Hospital in Shatin. Long, tall Jered Kok now worked for the Social Welfare Department, and Ben Yeung worked in an import-export company that often required him to travel into China. Each of these men now had a wife and young children. But they were willing to give numerous hours to organize and manage the centers. We could not have functioned without their valuable help, and we reflected with wonder at how God had used Lyn's simple Sunday school classes to prepare these men for this important work.

In March 1988, the first families moved into the new Po Lam Estate in Junk Bay. After four years of applications, negotiations, and red tape, the housing manager finally gave us our keys on April 18. The Po Lam Baptist Church and Elderly Center opened on July 16. We held classes of every kind: cooking, English, sewing, music, flower-arranging, Chinese writing. We invited Christian doctors to give talks: "How to Care for Your Body in Retirement Years." We sponsored outings and picnics, and even short trips into China. We also held Bible classes and invited center members to attend services at the church.

Miranda Law, who had prior experience in the Kwai Shing Center, came to work as our center supervisor in Po Lam. One of Miranda's friends wrote an inadvertently amusing recommendation which Lyn tucked away as a reminder that the level of English in Hong Kong was rather less than consistent. The letter attested that "Miss Law is a pessimistic lady and can face difficulties situation with a strong mind. She can see everything for a whole picture, not only her own. And in conclusion: she is rich of feeling, objective, pessimistic, and patience." Pessimistic or not, Miranda was a persevering, efficient supervisor, who swiftly recruited a team to lead the center.

Wo Lok Baptist pulled together to support the new church plant. Thirteen members volunteered to go to Po Lam to help start the new church. Since they were among the oldest and most mature Christians at Wo Lok, we were confident they would form a good church-planting team. We held a commissioning service for them on August 28. For two evenings, a large group of Wo Lok young people made the trip over the low mountain to Junk Bay. They tried to visit every home in the Po Lam Estate to invite the residents to our new church.

On September 4, 1988, Po Lam Baptist Church held its first worship service on Sunday morning, with thirty-six attending. On February 26, 1989, our three churches joined together for a landmark celebration: the tenth anniversary of Wo Lok, the independence of Shun On, and the dedication of Po Lam. For the past five years, Wo Lok and Shun On had been celebrating the Lord's Table together. The last joint communion service was held in December. At its conclusion, Pastor Teddy had us all stand in a circle around the auditorium and join hands as we sang the closing hymn. There were many tears as we realized how much we all meant to each other.

Looking around the circle of faces, Lyn and I knew how hard it would be to leave Shun On church. Time seemed to be passing ever more swiftly. Five years at Shun On had rushed by. Our children had grown and left Hong Kong. We had planted two churches, and it was already time to consider starting another church. Meanwhile, the 1997 handover was drawing nearer.

"CHAIRMAN'S TOMB AND EMPEROR'S PALACE
FACE EACH OTHER ACROSS THE SQUARE. . . .
EACH AND EVERY MARBLE STAIRCASE
COVERS HEAPS OF BONES BENEATH,
FROM THE EAVES OF SUCH FINE BUILDINGS
FRESH RED BLOOD DROPS EVERYWHERE."[1]

Beijing Street Voices

CHAPTER 21

THE DRAGON ROARS

For the people of Hong Kong, the year 1997 loomed like a storm cloud darkening over the colony. But for the Chinese in the mainland, the handover did not hold the same significance—how could they lose freedom they had never had? Instead, in the late 1980s, Chinese students began to clamor for the rights they lacked.

Over the last century, students in China had longed for and periodically worked for democracy. At the end of World War I, Chinese students, bitterly disappointed by the signed treaties, staged large demonstrations. On May 4, 1919, student representatives from thirteen universities in Peking[2] met, drawing up a plan of action expressed in five resolutions. According to historian Jonathan Spence, 3,000 students assembled at Tiananmen Square, defying police orders prohibiting public assembly.[3] They marched through the city, clashing violently with the police. One student was killed, and many were injured or arrested.

Decades later, Chinese people, particularly students, looked on the fourth of May as a day of commemoration. In May of 1989, students would stage another demonstration of their hopes for freedom and democracy, but this demonstration would end with even greater bloodshed. If in the 1980s a cloud hung ominously over Hong Kong, a far darker storm was fermenting on the Chinese mainland.

When Lyn and I took advantage of our 1988 Easter holiday break from the Bible college to fly to China, we had no sense of the horror that would be unleashed the next year. In contrast to our first visit to China a decade before, it was now relatively easy to travel on the mainland as tourists. We spent three days in Shanghai, staying at the Peace Hotel on the famous Bund, the street beside the Yangtze River harbor. On Easter Sunday, we visited the People's Park, talking for several hours with university students who came to practice English in the park's "English Corner."

The next day we took a four-hour train ride across the fertile farmlands of China's Zhejiang Province to the beautiful city of Hangzhou. The cherry blossoms were just beginning to bloom as we climbed a nearby mountain to visit a Buddhist temple over 1,600 years old. We flew out of Hangzhou airport, built by the Chinese to welcome President Nixon in 1972. It was fascinating to visit a place often called to our minds by news accounts and personal reports from students and church members.

Lyn and I wanted to visit China as often as possible in the next years to learn as much as we could about the world's largest country, particularly how the church was growing there. We realized again the need to learn Mandarin if we were to be able to communicate in most parts of the mainland. As the country had grown more open, it had been possible for our coworkers Bill Reid and Carson Fremont to make regular witnessing trips to China. They had seen many people come to Christ and others grow in the Lord during their countless visits. I still dreamed that CBTC, once HKBBI, might send Hong Kong disciples to China.

In November, Dave Pardini and I made a four-day trip to Beijing. Dave was a close colleague who had helped pastor Shun

On Baptist Church during some of Lyn's and my furloughs. He had arrived in Hong Kong with his wife, Peggy, in July 1982. Later, he would assume a position of leadership at the Bible college. Dave has a brilliant mind, and I particularly savored his company on this trip. In Beijing, we rode subways and buses so crowded we could not even raise our hands from our sides. We wandered through the Forbidden City and stood in awe of the vastness of Tiananmen Square. We were allowed to climb the steps and stand where Mao had stood when he proclaimed the Peoples' Republic as the new government of China in 1949. We stayed in the Beijing Hotel and gazed out at the wide streets below. Little did we realize that the streets and hotel would resound with gunfire in just seven months.

When Dave and I returned to Hong Kong, we found the colony peculiarly on edge. Following Britain's 1984 treaty with China, Hong Kong's 5.4 million people were particularly sensitive to any news from across the border on the mainland. In 1987, students in some Chinese cities had taken to the streets, calling for democracy and reform. The *International Herald Tribune* described the government's suppression of the demonstrations: "The student protests not only failed to move China further toward reform, but have prompted the leadership to clamp down. This has shattered the expectations many in Hong Kong had for their future after 1997. Many people are deeply demoralized."[4]

By the spring of 1989, Christians in Hong Kong were disturbed by accounts of increasing persecution of the church in China. At least twenty-one Christian leaders arrested in 1983 were still serving prison sentences four years after their arrests. In 1987, three itinerant evangelists were arrested in central China. In Sichuan Province and northern China, members of house churches were called in and detained by police. Once in jail, Christian worshipers had their heads shaved to further humiliate them. Over 100 Christians in Henan Province were imprisoned for evangelism—or as the Communists termed it—"illegal activities." Even as religious leaders were thrown in jail, Chinese lead-ers continually reassured the world that China's constitution allowed freedom of religion. Eager to continue economic rela-tions and to encourage any mention of democracy, the United States and Britain accepted the claims at face value.

As 1997 drew closer, the two million Hong Kong residents who had been born in mainland China and had fled the country to escape Communist persecution grew increasingly distressed at the thought of returning to Communist rule. Some reacted by demonstrating, and protests began to erupt in Hong Kong again—unheard of since the riots of 1967. A mob surrounded Sir David Wilson, Youde's successor as governor of Hong Kong, and blocked his car from leaving the Legislative Council building in Central District.[5]

Thousands began to leave the colony for any country to which they could somehow procure a visa—or even gain illegal entry. "One third of those polled say they want to immigrate," reported the *Hong Kong Standard*.[6]

But Chinese persecution did not ease. The very Christian movement which Bill Reid and Carson Fremont had witnessed on their frequent visits across the border was drawing the wrath of Communist authorities. The June 13, 1988, *Herald Tribune* reported, "The Chinese police raided an underground seminary and arrested several Protestant preachers in recent months in a campaign to halt a growing evangelical movement in China. Chi-nese Christians say they are being harassed, pressured, and perse-cuted. One man was suspended from a tree branch and beaten."[7]

In response, the emerging Chinese church in Hong Kong grew even stronger. Many were determined to stay in the colony and serve the Lord Christ there. They were propagating the Gospel more enthusiastically than ever before. Lyn and I felt honored to serve in the colony at this crucial time, helping to start new churches and leading the Bible college in the training of Christian workers.

But stories of persecution only accelerated the "brain drain" in the rest of Hong Kong, as intellectuals, businessmen, and factory workers alike fled the colony in search of a more secure future. Since the 1984 treaty, over 100,000 had already left Hong Kong, and 50,000 more were preparing to go soon, according to an article in *Time* magazine.[8]

Then, on April 15, 1989, Hu Yao-bang, the former secretary-general of the Communist Party of China, died suddenly of a heart attack. Students in Beijing immediately seized his death as an opportunity to press the government to move toward democratic reforms.[9] On April 17, thousands of students rallied in Tiananmen Square. The next night, showing bravery unparalleled under Communist rule in China, students staged sit-ins at Communist Party headquarters.

With Hu Yao-bang's funeral approaching on April 22, and the ever-sensitive May 4 day of commemoration just days away, the government forbade demonstrations and ordered the police to cordon off the square. Students knelt on the steps of the Great Hall of the People and, in time-honored Chinese practice, begged Premier Li Peng to come out and talk to them. When he refused, many of the students began a hunger strike.

On May 4, 100,000 students marched in Beijing. The square became a vast campsite, filled with the blankets, sleeping bags, and makeshift tents of 3,000 hunger strikers. They lay surrounded by tens of thousands of onlookers, while television cameras broadcast the scene around the world. Over the next week, many hunger strikers grew progressively weaker, and ambulance crews struggled through the crowds to reach those students who were at the point of death.[10]

By May 17, galvanized by the scenes of the fasting students, over one million Chinese had come to Beijing to assemble in the square. As the student demonstrations intensified, Hong Kong watched, transfixed. On May 20, the students of Hong Kong could watch no longer. On Hong Kong Island, 50,000 people streamed through the streets—in spite of a raging typhoon that brought 90 mile per hour winds and lashing rains—to protest in front of the New China News Agency, which served as an unofficial Chinese "embassy" in Hong Kong.

The following day, the *South China Morning Post* reported on the protest: "Hundreds of thousands of Hong Kong residents voted with their feet to express solidarity with the Beijing students in an historic march, demanding the resignation of Chinese Premier Li Peng."[11] The crowd was estimated at up to 600,000, the largest demonstration in Hong Kong's history.

On the same day, May 20, the Chinese government ordered Tiananmen Square cleared. The next day, more than one million Chinese citizens defied martial law and successfully blocked soldiers attempting to enter central Beijing. For two weeks, the people of Beijing united against the soldiers, raising barricades, forming human chains, and persuading the hesitant young soldiers not to fire on their own people.

Angered by the demonstrators' persistence and the soldiers' reluctance to enforce martial law, the government brought in the non-Mandarin-speaking troops of the Twenty-seventh Army. Since the men of the Twenty-seventh were older than the teenaged recruits and were mostly of peasant background, they felt little in common with the young students from the Chinese capital. They spoke a different dialect and could not understand the protestors, who pleaded, "The people should not shoot the people."[12] Late on the night of June 3, the army struck. Heavy tanks smashed through the makeshift barricades, crushing the protestors under them.

Thousands of soldiers proceeded down the streets, pouring machine-gun fire into the crowds. Reaching Tiananmen Square early on Sunday morning, June 4, the troops surrounded the exits to the square, and turned off all the lights.[13] "After protracted and anguished debates, the remaining students and demonstrators decided to leave. As they walked out in bedraggled but orderly form, troops and tanks overran their encampments," writes Jonathan Spence.[14]

In the following chaos, the army gunned down the unarmed students and citizens. The screams of the dying reverberated through the square, and the darkness was pierced by flames rising from the wreckage of the barricades and from grisly piles of human bodies. Hospitals were overwhelmed by the numbers of dead and wounded but, in many cases, doctors and nurses were forbidden by the army to treat civilian casualties. Even the doctors were slain in the streets as they knelt beside the wounded.[15]

On June 4, Hong Kong reporters from four television networks broadcasted live from Beijing. On that Sunday morning in our apartment, Lyn and I watched many of the sickening scenes in our small living-dining room. The networks ran the same footage over and over again, pictures of Chinese soldiers with guns and tanks slaughtering close to 3,000 people. The students' bodies lay everywhere, tangled in the wreckage of tents, of bicycles they had mounted in their haste to escape. Some had been pulverized by tanks, others shot, still others bayoneted in the stomach. The same Tiananmen Square that Lyn and I had so recently visited ran red with blood.

After watching the mayhem on television, Lyn and I took the bus over the mountain to Po Lam Baptist Church in Junk Bay. The church service was a time of worship, but it was a time of mourning as well. The believers stood around us, many of them weeping. All over the city, people talked of the momentous events in subdued tones.

Lyn and I rode the subway back to Nathan Road. But we couldn't muscle our way off the train because of the throngs filling the platform. By afternoon, silence had been replaced by anger. Over a million Hong Kong people—more than one sixth of Hong Kong's entire population—held a massive rally that brought the entire city to a standstill.[16] The city was gripped with rage and sorrow at what reporters all over the world were calling the Beijing Massacre. In some parts of Central District on the island, it was impossible to walk. Yet, despite the vast crowds, there was not a single arrest or reported injury.

Hong Kong people now demanded that Britain cancel its 1984 treaty with China. Britain not only refused to make any changes, Prime Minister Thatcher made the startling statement that she expected China to honor its agreement to treat Hong Kong well. China weighed in with the statement that those in Hong Kong demonstrating for democracy were lawbreakers subject to imprisonment or death. The words of the 1984 treaty—that freedoms of person, speech, movement, strike, and religious belief would be "ensured by law in the Hong Kong Special Administrative Region"—seemed almost farcical. Rather than offering any enforcement of these rights, Britain warned that it might give up Hong Kong *before* 1997. If the people of Hong Kong had felt betrayed before, then this further treachery was insufferable.

Britain's foreign secretary, Sir Geoffrey Howe, visited Hong Kong in July to try to bring some reassurance to the people there. Thousands blocked the roads from the airport to Government House, where he was to stay. They held up signs with just one word in Chinese and English: "SHAME!"

Meanwhile, in China, the Communist government denied outright that the massacre had taken place, despite documentation by newspapers, television, and books such as Melinda Liu's *Beijing Spring* and Donald Morrison's definitive *Massacre in Beijing*.[17] Lyn and I personally saw pictures—taken both in Tiananmen Square and in Beijing hospitals—of several hundred bodies. For the people of Hong Kong, all hopes of China becoming more open and democratic had been crushed. The Dragon Empire had dropped its friendly mask, revealing jaws stained with the blood of its own people. In all our years living in the shadow of the Dragon Empire, Lyn and I had never imagined such atrocities would occur. With heavy hearts, we returned to Ashland, Ohio, in July 1989 for our fifth furlough.

LONDON, 1992

"The loss of Hong Kong was a national humiliation
that was followed by a number of unequal treaties
which were unacceptable to the Chinese people."

Ma Yu-zhen, Chinese Ambassador to the Court of St. James, London, England

CHAPTER 22

GARDEN ESTATE

In June 1990, we returned from furlough to an overheated city, 90°F with humidity of 93 percent. The heat shimmered in waves off the hot, concrete buildings. It would remain that hot and humid every day until the end of September. When we returned to our Ferry Street apartment, Lyn and Brent laughed and told me they knew we were back home in Hong Kong—hopping out of the taxi, they had seen four rats before they even reached the front door of our apartment building. In the heat, the pests of Hong Kong thrived. Rats ran in the streets among the garbage; moths and other insects infested our groceries, no matter how tightly we sealed our food.

The Hong Kong of 1990 was also overheated politically. More than 1,000 people were leaving the city every week. Emigration jumped to 60,000 people in 1990 and continued to grow. The apartment building where we lived had six apartments on each floor. During our furlough, three of the other five families on our floor sold their apartments and left Hong Kong. On July 25, over 45,000 people lined up at the Immigration Department in one day to apply for permits to move to Britain.

On Sunday, June 3, more than 100,000 protestors choked the streets of Hong Kong to mark the first anniversary of the massacre in Beijing. Clad in black, the somber protestors waved banners reading, "The people will never forget!" Their words were an ironic reference to the fact that the so-called "People's Liberation Army" had slaughtered more than 3,000 people in the square in Beijing. On the night of June 4, more than 100,000 packed Victoria Park on Hong Kong Island. In spite of the oppressive heat, they held an emotional candlelight vigil. Just as "9/11" is recognized by Americans as shorthand for the tragic September 11 attacks on the Twin Towers, June 4 had become enshrined in the Hong Kong psyche as the date of the infamous Beijing Massacre.

News from China only exacerbated the political tensions. The situation was not growing any easier for Christians in China. Earlier that year in Guangzhou, formerly called Canton, Communist police had raided a well-known Christian church. Fifty men had stormed into the parsonage of Pastor Samuel Lam, ransacking his home and seizing everything of value—Bibles, church offerings, even the organ. After dragging a group of believers to the police station, they interrogated Pastor Lam for twenty-one hours.

Lyn and I, however, were thankful for the faithful, growing church in Hong Kong, which was boldly proclaiming the Gospel as the answer for Hong Kong's restless generation facing the 1990s. We felt privileged to work with some of the finest Christians in the world. Teddy and Jennifer were now in their eleventh year of faithful service at Wo Lok. At the end of our furlough, Kristi and her husband, Walter, had presented us with our second grandchild, Walter Gordon Hackney, born April 28, 1990. When we returned from furlough, Teddy and Jennifer's growing children brought extra joy into our lives, and helped alleviate the pain of being so far from our own grandchildren. Two-year-old Timothy insisted on piggy-back rides every Sunday morning at the Po Lam church.

Before leaving for furlough, Teddy and I had applied for a site to start a fourth church. It was for a day nursery in an area called Garden Estate, one subway stop west of Wo Lok Baptist. The site was scheduled to be ready in the summer of 1989. Garden Estate would house 14,000 people in four buildings, each more than thirty stories high. The field council appointed Pastor Teddy and me to lead a team to start Wo Lok's third daughter church there.

In the late 1980s, it was apparent that God was beginning to give great fruit in church-planting efforts all over the city. People were coming to the Lord in greater numbers than ever before, many driven by fear of what might happen in 1997—would their businesses suffer, would they lose their riches and their freedoms? Some even feared for their lives. Though we did not understand all of the factors, we were thankful for what God was doing, and we wanted to start as many churches as possible.

The Garden Estate premises would be different from our first three churches. The site the government wanted to lease to us had ten rooms and an area of 5,200 square feet—almost three times the size of each of our first three church-plants. The site location was ideal, for Garden Estate was being built just across the street from a large MTR station. We were accustomed to dealing with the Housing Authority, but a different government department, the Housing Society, ran Garden Estate. The Housing Society promised that if we put in offices, partitions, the electrical system, and air conditioning, they would pay for the major construction work on walls, windows, ceilings, floors, and bathrooms. This was far more than had been promised us in our first three centers.

Pastor Teddy and the Wo Lok deacons were enthusiastic about the project, which was estimated to cost $30,000. The Wo Lok church set a goal of raising $15,000 while we were in the United States on furlough. We set the same target, asking the Lord to bring in $15,000 during our furlough. Wo Lok raised their share first, but on the last Sunday of our furlough, North Royalton Baptist Church in Ohio gave over $6,000 in one day toward the project. All of the needed funds were now in hand.

By October 1990, the buildings in Garden Estate were completed on the outside, and workmen were finishing up interior work. We would not receive the keys for another month or two, and we suspected that we would not be able to open the church and day nursery before January 1991. We still needed to hire a supervisor and staff of ten for this project.

October 14, 1990, marked a turning point in our church-planting work in Hong Kong. On that cool, unusually beautiful autumn afternoon—such a relief from the heat of the summer—Pastor Teddy, Pastor Caleb, and I baptized twenty-three people into the memberships of Wo Lok, Shun On, and Po Lam Baptist churches. As each of the new members gave his or her testimony, Lyn and I realized how far we had come from that day when we first arrived in Kwun Tong, not knowing a single person, and never having planted a church before.

We had worked for many years, mainly with young people, but since the Po Lam Elderly Center had opened, we were seeing older people come to the Lord, too. It was just as thrilling to hear their testimonies. One woman, Mrs. Cheui, told how she had worshipped idols, but came to Christ after a believer shared the Gospel with her in the hospital during her husband's long illness. Now, in addition to giving out tracts and witnessing near her home, she witnessed to patients every week at several hospitals.

The testimony of Mrs. Leung, from Shun On, was particularly powerful. When Mrs. Leung's thirteen-year-old son was dying of bone cancer several years earlier, Kitty, a nurse from Wo Lok, had led him to the Lord. As Mrs. Leung saw the great change in her son and the peace with which he faced his death, Kitty also led her to Christ. Breaking down as she spoke, Mrs. Leung whispered though her tears, "Now I know that some day I will see my son again in heaven."

As the ceremony concluded, people showered flowers upon

their newly baptized friends, a favorite custom among Hong Kong Christians, and took dozens of pictures. It was an afternoon long to be remembered.

That same month, in the midst of our joy for the new members, Lyn's mother, Anne Alexander, developed acute pneumonia. She was eighty-six, and knowing that her quality of life had been poor for a number of years, Lyn and I began to pray along with other family members that the Lord would soon call her home. Her "Promotion Day" came on November 12, 1990. A few days later, family and friends gathered for a memorial service in Rockford, Illinois, led by Lyn's pastor-brother, Paul. We had guessed when we said goodbye to her in May 1990, at the end of our last furlough, that we would not see her again until heaven. Though we mourned her death, we were grateful for her release.

For the rest of 1990, Lyn and I put our hearts into finalizing the Garden Estate project. In a radical departure from our first two church-planting efforts, Teddy and the Wo Lok church deacons wanted to send a large team to Garden Estate. They hoped to get a faster start on the new church and also to create space in the Wo Lok auditorium again so that they could reach more people in their own area. For several months, Pastor Teddy asked people to pray about who should go to help start Garden Estate.

When Garden Estate Baptist Church opened on January 6, 1991, a group of forty-eight believers were in attendance. Wo Lok had formed this team from its best members to help start their third daughter church. They did not plan to invite people from the area until the interior renovation work was done. The church-planting team would have several valuable months to pray and plan together.

Lyn and I rejoiced as we sang a Chinese version of Beethoven's "Joyful, Joyful We Adore Thee" at the service. This was the fourth time we had worked with Pastor Teddy and Jennifer Cheng to start a new church, and we realized we were blessed by the unique partnership. Philip Yim, who had been an assistant pastor at Wo Lok Baptist since the previous summer, was to lead the new church at Garden Estate, while Teddy and I acted as advisers and supporting preachers.

But early in 1991, the Housing Society shocked us by saying that because of "budget shortfalls," they would hand us a stripped-down center. This was a government that had seen nineteen budget surpluses in the previous twenty years! Now, we would have to put in the walls, windows, ceilings, floors, and bathrooms—all work which the Housing Society had previously promised to complete themselves, in a signed contract.

Our contractor told us that due to these changes, we would now need a minimum of $137,000 to get the nursery open. We had $42,000 on hand. In meetings with the government, they told us that they would give us until June 1 to get the project operational. Gaining the needed approvals from the Housing Society, Social Welfare Department, Buildings and Lands, and Fire Services would eat up three months of that precious time. So we had only two or three months to solve the problem of funding.

This was the biggest challenge we had ever faced in our church-planting work. We asked our friends in the United States to pray urgently that the Lord would give us great wisdom in quickly dealing with these obstacles. As I prayed and thought about the problem, I had a strong conviction that we should not make a direct appeal to the churches in the United States for these funds. I met with Teddy to discuss the situation.

"Let me say something first," Teddy began. "Please don't ask the churches in North America for the money we need. Please give a chance to our Christians first." It seemed that the Lord had given us both one mind, and we were assured He was going before us.

Construction was completed by the end of June. The final cost of the project came to about $129,000. In a great answer to prayer, the money was all in hand. Even without a direct appeal, loving people in the United States gave $27,000. All the rest of the money came from Hong Kong. Wo Lok and its three daughter churches rose to the challenge when they gave $71,000 in love offerings in five months—doubling their normal giving! The Hong Kong churches' giving had remarkably demonstrated their independence.

We received an official government license for the nursery on August 1. We hired Mrs. Mabel Mak as the nursery supervisor. She was a Christian from Wo Lok who had previously worked in several centers, including Po Lam. Her husband, Stanley, had been one of the first believers at the Wo Lok church. She proved to be an excellent supervisor—efficient, and always pleasant to work with. Many visitors began to attend Sunday services at Garden Estate, and the team from Wo Lok visited every home in the estate with invitations to our new church.

We held the Garden Estate Baptist Church dedication service in November 1991. Several hundred people gathered on a beautiful fall day for the occasion. The dedication was the culmination of a fall season that had seen growth in all of our churches. The four churches averaged 321 in attendance in October. The Lord had brought us a long, long way from the day when two young men gathered for a service in our Kwun Tong living room.

That afternoon, the churches joined for an outdoor baptism. We soon ran out of the 400 printed bulletins, but much more important than attendance were the lives God had changed. We baptized twenty-two into the churches, and each one gave a testimony of how Christ had brought new life. Some were young; some were old. Some were smiling, some cried tears of emotion and joy. They all stayed around talking, laughing, and taking pictures until after dark. Brent, who was living with us and working as editor of the Inchcape Company magazine, was amazed by the crowd. He had never seen so many people attend a baptism in Hong Kong.

In the spring, when the nursery school opened, Lyn relished teaching basic English to the children. One day, she accompanied 100 children, their teachers, and many parents and grandparents on an outing to Ocean Park. The buses wended their way through heavy traffic, crossing under the harbor and passing through the Aberdeen Tunnel to the south side of Hong Kong Island. The children enjoyed the whales and dolphins, but Lyn enjoyed interacting with their mothers even more. The nursery was full, with many children on a waiting list.

That spring also brought a growing crime wave to Hong Kong. Some top Hong Kong policemen thought the Chinese government was deliberately allowing—even encouraging—heavily armed criminals to cross the border into the colony. Gangs of criminals called triads ran organized crime networks. The results were appalling.

On April 24, 1992, police broke into an apartment where robbers of a jewelry store were hiding. The thieves fought their way out using machine guns and grenades, provoking what the *South China Morning Post* called "the most violent gun battle in Hong Kong's history" less than a quarter mile west of our college. Seventeen were injured and several died. On May 5, the bus on which I was riding home was stopped by another wild gun battle a mile south of the college. But in these uncertain times, it seemed there was more of a hunger for the Gospel than at any other time in our twenty-seven years in Hong Kong.

The prosperous city was also a great contrast to the poverty-filled place we had first seen in the 1960s. We had a vivid example of this when I joined Mabel Mak, the nursery supervisor, to interview applicants for a janitor's job. The woman we chose had only a seventh-grade education, yet she would receive a starting salary that was higher than my current missionary salary. We were glad to see so many members in our churches earning good salaries, a marked contrast to when we had first arrived in the colony.

In July 1993, Garden Estate Baptist Church voted to call Samuel Wong as pastor, and his wife, Rachel, as Christian Education director. They were both graduates of CBTC and had started their friendship on a college trip to Israel. Lyn and I had watched with delight as Samuel and Rachel ate lunch together in Corinth, walked together in Galilee, and talked together in Rome. Soon after we returned to Hong Kong, they came to our tiny apartment one Sunday evening to tell us of their engagement. Now, five years later, we were thankful that they had chosen to come to Garden Estate.

Pastor Wong and his committee set January 1, 1995, as a target date for the church's independence. As the Garden Estate church plant slowly grew, we witnessed one of the most remarkable answers to prayer that we ever saw. Mak Chi-chung was a young man from the Wo Lok church who had volunteered to help start Garden Estate church. Chi-chung's ten-year-old brother, Chi-fai, died after a fall on the school playground back in 1981. Now Chi-chung was married with two sons of his own.

After Chi-fai's death, Teddy, Jennifer, Lyn, and I had often visited Mr. and Mrs. Mak, who attended Wo Lok for a while before dropping away. We mentioned their names in our prayer letters. People wrote to tell us they were praying for the Maks more than for any other prayer request in our years in Hong Kong. Chi-chung and others continued to witness patiently to his parents. Ten years passed, then fifteen, without the Maks responding to the Gospel.

Then, after Chi-chung and his family starting attending Garden Estate, his father was diagnosed with terminal cancer. In his last months on earth, Mr. Mak's heart finally softened, and he came to Christ. Shortly after her husband accepted Christ, Mrs. Mak also received the Lord. Twenty years after Chi-fai's sudden death had grieved us all and set us praying for the Mak family's salvation, God had finally answered our prayers. We were humbled as we realized the extent of God's patience and mercy. As ever, He worked in His own time, opening people's hearts long after many had forgotten.

Around the same time, we received a phone call from Lyn's sister telling us that Lyn's dad, Fred Alexander, had gone to be with the Lord on March 23, 1994. He died at eighty-eight in the nursing section of the retirement home in Rockford, Illinois, where he had lived for twelve years. He had been a great influence in our lives, and we would miss him dearly. Lyn's earliest memories were of the godly example of her father. We were genuinely glad that "Pop" was now free from suffering and limitations, but we sensed a period of change coming in our lives.

On April 7, 1994, Garden Estate hit a record attendance of eighty-four, and the church committee recommended moving the date of the independence service up to July 1994. The committee was filled with mature, wise people, and I agreed with their recommendation. The church unanimously voted in favor, and the service was held on July 3, six months earlier than expected. In 1990, we had asked friends to pray that God would raise up an independent church in Garden Estate. Four years later, He had answered these prayers.

All four churches which we had helped to plant—Wo Lok, Shun On, Po Lam, and Garden Estate—were thriving under Chinese leadership. God had truly watered the seeds we had planted. As Garden Estate continued to grow, Lyn and I realized we would not be needed there much longer. Though we did not know it then, the remaining years of the decade would hold a major transition, not only for Hong Kong, but for us as well.

1995 – 2001

TRANSITION YEARS

HONG KONG, MARCH 18, 1993

"CHRIS PATTEN WILL BE CONDEMNED IN HONG KONG'S HISTORY
AS A MAN OF GUILT."

Chinese government official, Lu Ping
South China Morning Post

CHAPTER 23

GROWTH IN THE COLLEGE

In 1992, Chris Patten became the last governor of Hong Kong. The Prime Minister of England, John Major, regretted the way Britain had handled negotiations with China, and urged Patten to push for a last-minute expansion of democratic representation. Immediately upon arriving in Hong Kong, Patten made plans to have part of the legislature elected by the people. But the largest number of Hong Kong's people who ever voted under the British (in the Legislative Council elections of 1995) was only 11 percent of those who would have been eligible in a normal democracy.[1] By stopping short of real elections, the British gave the Communists an excuse to prevent real elections after the handover.

Still, Patten's popularity in Hong Kong soared, provoking the Chinese mainland press to vilify him. They hurled absurd taunts like third-graders on a school playground, labeling Patten "the criminal who will be condemned for a thousand generations, the serpent, the whore of the East, and the tango dancer."[2] Throughout his short term, Patten would battle time and the intransigent Chinese government to pass even a handful of his reforms.

Like Patten, Lyn and I were campaigning for nationals to

take leadership before the 1997 handover—of the college and churches, if not the territory. We were also fighting against time, though we did not know it, for in the early 1990s, Lyn began to have trouble organizing her classes at China Baptist Theological College. Students noticed that she seemed unfocused, or struggled with words. Lyn and I had always loved the hearty singing at the daily chapels. But during church services, she stopped singing. She began to speak Cantonese less and less. Since her conversational Cantonese had always been better than mine, I was surprised. A few times I urged her, "Honey, if you stop using your Cantonese, you will lose it." She didn't answer. Despite these ominous signs, 1990–1994 was a period of great productivity for us.

The independence service for Garden Estate had been a milestone. Garden Estate was our fourth and final church plant. Now that we had seen the three Wo Lok churches become independent, we also yearned to see the China Baptist Theological College make the same transition. The college's history in the last ten years had been one of growth, just like that of the churches. Since the "Miracle of 1980," we had quadrupled the size of our facilities, constructing two dormitories, a faculty apartment, a well-functioning and well-equipped office complex, adequate classrooms, a chapel, and a library. Before 1984, we were fortunate to add one student a year; after 1989, we never again had fewer than twenty students.

The Lord sent Chinese pastors to form the core of college personnel. Pastor Ng of Evangel Baptist Church became our student counselor, and Pastor Leo Lam of Kwai Shing Baptist became our director of internship. Pastor Teddy accepted the position of dean of students, and together with our academic dean, Norm Barnard, and assistant to the president, Sue Farley, they formed an invaluable group of advisors who served as the college's administrative committee.

As Garden Estate became more independent, Lyn and I were

able to spend more time with the CBTC students. I taught three or four courses on theology, hermeneutics, and Old Testament books every semester. Lyn taught one or two English classes, which were crucial to the students training to be pastors. Chinese pastors urged us to continue to put a priority on English, because students needed to be able to comprehend theological reference books, only a limited number of which were available in Chinese. A shortage of theological reference texts in the Chinese language continues to this day.

The faculty worked hard to make the college a family rather than just an academic experience. Each school year began with a student-faculty retreat, often in the rugged peninsula in the eastern New Territories. The program included volleyball, archery, and long hikes and runs in the hills. Despite the faculty's valiant efforts, they were usually unable to beat the students in basketball.

For several years, I had won three-mile races at the retreat— until Timothy Ng arrived. He had worked for Hong Kong's Fire Services for several years and was in superb shape. At one race, he ran beside me for several miles, casually chatting as easily as if he were sitting on the couch in the student lounge. Then, with a half mile to go, he smiled and said, "Excuse me, Pastor Hon, I'm going to run on ahead for a while." I could only stare in amazement as he accelerated out of sight.

Lyn, with her caring heart and hospitable nature, had always been an unofficial "mother" to the students, and her work went a long way to making the college a family. Whenever there was trouble, Lyn would reach out to the students, particularly the girls. One girl, an orphan, broke into tears after Lyn hugged her, saying, "No one ever hugged me before." Because our apartment was so tiny, we had no room to entertain students, so we visited their homes instead. During the Chinese New Year, Lyn and I devoted our afternoons to visiting students, following the Chinese tradition of visiting family and friends. Many had unsaved family members, but we always received a warm welcome.

* * *

Most of the students had never been out of Hong Kong, and we wanted them to develop a wider vision of God's work in the world. Past trips to other mission fields had proved very successful in educating them. In December 1983, we had sent a team of six faculty and students to Manila: Norm and Louise Barnard, Pastor Teddy Cheng, Pastor Yeung of Heritage Baptist, and two students, Winnie Chu and Bill Kam. After visiting the Baptist Bible Seminary in Manila, the group flew to a student missions conference at Doane Baptist Bible College in Iloilo City. Eating fresh fruit as they rode on jeeps and trucks in Guimaras Island and Kabankalan was light years away from the CBTC campus in crowded Kowloon.

Our faculty also believed it was essential for our students to become familiar with the lands of the Bible that formed a background for all their studies. In the 1980s, we had organized several trips to Israel, Rome, and Greece, the first in 1986 as a celebration of the college's twentieth anniversary. We challenged each student to raise half the cost of his trip, and I asked God to provide the other half. Friends in the United States and Hong Kong gave what was needed.

On the 1985 trip, our group of teachers, pastors, and students flew to Rome. We were especially moved as we stood in the cold, damp, dark remains of the Mamertine Prison. With only a hole in the ceiling for an entrance, this forbidding rocklike cave seemed an unlikely place for Paul to write the joyful letter to the Philippians. I noticed Teddy standing against one wall, completely silent, pondering the words Paul had written while in chains: "Rejoice in the Lord always." Teddy, like the other Hong Kong believers, was moved by the persecution Paul and other Christians had faced throughout history.

In Israel, we stayed just inside the old walled city of Jerusalem. Pastor Teddy led Sunday morning worship on the top of the Mount of Olives. In the Judean desert, Norm Barnard led us in devotions at En Gedi, beside the waterfall where David escaped from King Saul. We sailed across the Sea of Galilee with the sun falling in bright sheets across the water and stood in awe at the top of Megiddo. It was extraordinary to walk in the very footsteps of the Bible, to see Christian history made vividly real.

In Athens, Lyn led our devotional time in the marketplace where Paul had debated with the men of the city, and Bill Kam preached on top of Mars' Hill. After arriving home, the students expressed their gratitude: "We find no written or spoken words to fully express our appreciation. We just want you to know that this trip with you is so enjoyable and meaningful."

Lyn and I were touched by the letter of another student, Rachel Ma, who wrote:

> To Dearest Father and Mother of Israel, Pastor and Mrs. Hon,
>
> I thank God that he let me grow in CBTC to be your daughter for these four years. Also, I thank you so much for giving me a chance to go to Israel and receiving a wonderful gift that I have never experienced.
>
> Your Israel's child,
> Rachel Ma

The trip made such an impact on us all that we made a policy to visit the Bible lands every three years, so that each student would have the opportunity to go during his four years of college. In the next eighteen years, almost every student made the journey.

* * *

As I sat with Pastor Yeung Po-wan drinking coffee outside a shop in Athens on one of these Israel trips, he shared with me that the Lord was leading him to emigrate to the greater Toronto area in Canada, to start a church among Chinese refugees there. I was shocked.

Po-wan had become one of the outstanding leaders of

ABWE's work in Hong Kong. He served as pastor at Sunshine Baptist Church from 1968 to 1972. He then worked with Bill Commons, serving as Kwai Shing Baptist Church's first pastor from 1972 to 1977. He excelled as pastor of Heritage Baptist Church in Mei Foo, which Bob and Margaret Paswaters had started. Under Po-wan's leadership and vision from 1978 to 1989, Heritage grew into a strong church with over 300 people, starting two daughter churches. Po-wan also bolstered the faculty of CBTC, teaching many students how to preach.

In the Spring 2000 issue of the ABWE *Message,* Po-wan described how God changed his vision:

> In 1989, we moved to Toronto, Ontario, a city that 400,000 Chinese call home. By God's grace we started two churches. The mother church has completed a building program, and today the daughter church is also independent. My wife and I began praying for God's guidance for the next step in our lives. I realized the baton has now shifted to us who were led to Christ and trained by foreign missionaries. I have church planting in my blood. How can I be satisfied simply pastoring a church? In December 1998, Dr. Kempton asked me, "Would you pray about starting Chinese churches globally?"

Po-wan answered by agreeing to become ABWE's director of International Chinese Ministries.

Sitting in Athens that morning, I could not see at first how CBTC would go on without him. So many pastors had emigrated from Hong Kong that one poll in 1990 estimated more than half the colony's remaining pastors were under age thirty. His leaving would be a great loss. But I realized that as we neared the handover of Hong Kong to China, the Lord would lead different Christians in different ways. Soon after, I learned that our beloved dean of CBTC, Norm Barnard, also planned to leave Hong Kong, to become the president of Asia Baptist Theological Seminary, headquartered in Singapore.

CBTC's administration was now working toward the goal of becoming indigenous: making the college independent from ABWE and handing the presidency over to a local administrator by August 1995. We wanted CBTC to be independent well before the 1997 handover. The missionaries were encouraged by the attitude of our Chinese brothers. They urged us to drop the use of the term "indigenous," which would imply that only Chinese teachers would teach, and instead use the term "localized," which would mean using the best teacher available even if he happened to be a North American. The CBTC Board unanimously agreed to adopt the path to localization and to press ahead vigorously to relocate the campus.

A small hillside plot in the Shatin valley in the New Territories became the leading possibility for our new location. Shatin had been a quiet village in the 1960s, but it was now a booming satellite city with a population of 530,000.[3] The Huang family was considering selling their old village home in Shatin. On a hillside overlooking the city, the land was still surrounded by a swath of grass and trees, a rare commodity in greenery-starved Hong Kong. I had worked with James Huang at Calvary Baptist in the 1960s, and we were still good friends. If CBTC could buy the property, we could tear down the house and build three small buildings on the land. The board began to discuss buying the Huang property.

In order to raise up more potential Chinese leaders, Pastor Teddy suggested that we teach classes for laymen in local churches. We remembered the college's origins as an evening school in 1966, and how evening students had often been inspired to become full-time. Church members responded to Teddy's innovation, and by 1990 we had over 100 evening school students. From 1990–1994, I concentrated on teaching Theology in the evening school and putting deep concepts into simple terms.

In 1992, we finished writing the constitution for the college and were ready to register with the Hong Kong government so that the property could be turned over to a localized college board. But the real heart of the college was not paper and committees; rather it was the new Chinese graduates who entered the Lord's work every year. Winnie Chu (1986) became the Christian Education director at Heritage Baptist Church. Holly Poon (1987) worked as Christian Education director at Wo Lok Baptist and her classmate, Philip Yeung, specialized in prison ministry. P. K. Wong (1987) became senior pastor of Calvary Baptist, now a growing church of 300, with four daughter churches, two granddaughter churches, and another branch church to start that summer. Timothy Ng (1990) was an associate pastor at Heritage, another church of almost 300.

On October 14, 1993, Lyn and I rejoiced to see the college turned over to the new localized board. We were seeing the double blessing of our efforts—both in the churches and the college. Some goals remained, but CBTC was well on its way to independence. The board asked me to continue as president while the search continued for a Chinese president. They were hopeful of finding the right person within the next year or two. But though they continued to search, they were not yet satisfied they had found the man of the Lord's choice.

In the spring of 1994, our new academic dean, Dave Pardini, passed the final oral examination to receive his doctorate from Trinity Evangelical Divinity School in Chicago. When he returned to Hong Kong, we held a surprise "graduation" for him in the college chapel. We included everything we could think of: cap, gown, hood, a special cake with the message, "Congrats, Dr. Dave"—and a kiss from his wife, Peggy. The board appointed Dave to serve as acting president during our 1994-1995 furlough. Lyn and I were free to prepare for our return to Ohio.

I was grateful for the way the Lord had immensely prospered our work, but a shadow was cast over my joy as I noticed my wife becoming increasingly uneasy in her speech. She rarely spoke

Cantonese, seeming strangely unfocused. We had lived in the shadow of the Dragon Empire for many years, but now a more personal dragon was threatening.

HONG KONG, JULY 1, 1997

"AS THE RAIN CAME DOWN, THE END OF EMPIRE
IN THIS CORNER OF THE WORLD BEGAN. A TELEGRAM FLASHED
FROM GOVERNOR PATTEN TO LONDON: 'I HAVE RELINQUISHED
THE ADMINISTRATION OF THIS GOVERNMENT.
GOD SAVE THE QUEEN.'"

South China Morning Post

CHAPTER 24

PASSING THE TORCH

Lyn had always had a brilliant mind. She was the wordsmith of the family, the English teacher, the writer. She had served in so many different capacities, teaching students both in church and at the college, helping to maintain a lifeline to our supporters through her vivid letters, full of lively descriptions and meditative reflections. She had helped me to write, to teach, to think, and had pursued her own studies with zeal and insight. But at the end of 1994, Lyn's hold on language was slipping. Kristi and Lori told me that their mother's letters had begun to include misspellings and even grammar mistakes. For the woman the field council jokingly called "our unofficial grammarian," this was worrisome.

As we prepared for our 1994 furlough, I began to pack boxes to ship home to the States. I pulled down the suitcases for Lyn to pack her things. But when I came home at night, I noticed that although she had spread many things on the bed, she hadn't put anything in the suitcases. When the same pattern was repeated several days in a row, I began to realize that for some reason Lyn was unable to pack. I had to stay up much of the last night to pack her things.

As soon as we returned to Ashland, Ohio, in June 1994, I took Lyn to her physician. The doctor hoped Lyn's problem was something minor, such as a B-12 vitamin deficiency. But when there was no real improvement from B-12 shots, she sent us to a neurologist in nearby Mansfield. After a long examination, he ordered an MRI. We went to the Mansfield Hospital early on a chilly November morning. I felt claustrophobic as the nurses rolled Lyn into the massive machine, but she was peacefully listening to some of her favorite music.

As I sat in the waiting room, I really didn't know how to pray. The neurologist had eliminated many possibilities, and the remaining ones all seemed grim. The doctors were testing Lyn for a brain tumor. But if a tumor was ruled out, it was then likely that she had one of the memory-loss diseases. Even with that warning, I was not prepared for the diagnosis. The neurologist told me tests had ruled out other possibilities, and Lyn probably had early onset Alzheimer's disease. Alzheimer's is a progressive, degenerative, and incurable brain disorder that always ends in death. The neurologist also said that patients diagnosed with Alzheimer's in their seventies often lived for many years. But for reasons doctors do not understand, someone diagnosed at age sixty-five or younger usually only lives a few years. Lyn was only fifty-nine.

A strange peace came over me, that I would not have thought possible. The Lord was bringing our church planting and our teaching at CBTC to fulfillment just in time. It was clear to me that God was giving me a new assignment of caring for Lyn, and this would take precedence over anything in my life.

Because we had lived in Hong Kong for most of the previous thirty years, Lyn's neurologist advised us to return there after furlough, thinking Lyn might cope better in familiar surroundings. She wanted very much to return to Hong Kong, so we flew back into the colony on July 30, 1995, to an overwhelming welcome. We had missed the June 1994 CBTC graduation service, when over 900 people from many of ABWE's twenty-seven churches crowded into a rented auditorium to honor the six graduates. But now, almost all of CBTC's twenty-two students met us at the airport, along with friends from Po Lam Baptist and other churches.

I realized that our only hope to stay in Hong Kong was to live very near the college. We found a tiny flat on the twentieth floor of the building next to CBTC. After painting and buying furniture, we moved in. It was only a one-minute walk to the school. We could eat some meals at the college, and I hoped Lyn would be able to interact with the students and continue some part of her ministry.

The term started wonderfully, with the marriage of our son Brent to Clare Cochrane, an English girl who had grown up in Hong Kong. Their wedding took place at the Hong Kong Yacht Club on August 26, 1995. I was privileged to perform the ceremony, and I managed not to cry until the very end, when I tried to read the ancient Hebrew blessing in Numbers 6:24–26: "May the Lord bless you and watch over you."

As a special surprise, Kristi and our five-year-old grandson, Walter Gordon, had flown into Hong Kong without warning. When we took them to Brent's apartment, he was speechless. In the five days they stayed, we tried to show Walter Gordon everything we could in such a short time. Brent's cousin, Bill, came from Japan, and other friends came from Rome, London, San Francisco, and New York—not unusual at the wedding of a graduate of King George V School, which regularly had students from over forty countries.

But despite the joy of the wedding, my hopes of Lyn surviving in Hong Kong were soon dashed. She now exhibited eight or nine of the twelve "warning symptoms" for early onset Alzheimer's. She could no longer spell nor write; she could not cook or use the washing machine. She couldn't dial the phone, and most days she couldn't use the key in the door. She was not able to come up with the main words in sentences, so she substituted others. Sometimes they fit, sometimes they didn't. We bought a phone so that she could dial the college by pushing one button, and I came home several times a day to check on her. The doctor tried a new medicine called Cognex, but rather than helping Lyn, it nauseated her.

By Christmas, I realized we would not be able to stay in Hong Kong, and I began to pray that the Lord would enable us to finish out the current school year. I knew my first responsibility was to care for Lyn. I had no hesitancy at all in notifying the CBTC Board, the field council, and the ABWE Board of my resignation as the president of CBTC. I asked them to pray the Lord would help us stay until June 1996.

After Christmas, I took Lyn on the hydrofoil to Macao, the Portuguese colony forty miles down the coast. The weather was perfect, clear and sunny each day, and chilly and pleasant in the evenings. We took long walks, delighting in the thousands of Christmas lights shining all over Macao's streets and buildings. Lyn thanked me for "taking her away" and seemed to enjoy the trip as much as any vacation I could remember. This seemed a special gift from the Lord.

In February 1996, Teddy Cheng and Dave Pardini helped Lyn and me lead a group of thirty-five students on CBTC's fifth Israel trip. By now, Teddy was the dean of students and Dave was the academic dean. We had a smooth journey to Egypt, Jordan, and Israel, despite the ever-present danger in the Middle East. On Sunday morning, February 25, we were to journey into the wilderness of Judah. But I had to travel instead to the area near Jerusalem's Central Bus Station with Esther Lee, a student who had lost her plane ticket. Esther and I came on the scene just one hour after a suicide bomber had blown up a bus, killing twenty-five people. We watched bodies being pulled out of the wreckage and hundreds of Hasidic Jews shouting in anger at Prime Minister Peres, who had come to inspect the scene. It was a terrible reminder of the peace withheld from Jerusalem.

In spite of witnessing this horrific scene, this was our best trip to Israel. We were particularly privileged to have Kristi's husband, Walter Hackney, and our granddaughter, Anne, join the group of students and teachers. On one remarkable afternoon, we rode ski lifts 9,000 feet to the top of Mount Hermon. The Chinese students delighted to see snow for the first time in their lives, and we had snowball fights and sled races in the deep snow. The students stood in awe at the Sea of Galilee, Mount Sinai, and Jerusalem's Temple Mount, and said later these three places brought the Bible most alive. When we all planted a tree on a hill in Galilee, I realized this was a farewell of sorts to the college for Lyn and me.

* * *

In March, after we returned to Hong Kong, a series of three life-changing events occurred in ten days and took my breath away.

First, Teddy Cheng accepted the presidency of China Baptist Theological College. Caleb Shum agreed to become the academic dean, and Dave Pardini agreed to serve as vice-president during the transition. I would now be able to step down without anxiety. The Lord had provided three well-prepared men to lead the college past the 1997 handover and into the next century.

Second, in an extraordinary meeting with our Far Eastern administrator, Bill Commons, the field council recognized ABWE's achievement of all its major goals for the Hong Kong field to become indigenous. From 1952 to 1972, American missionaries started all of ABWE's first seven churches in Hong Kong. But since 1984, independent Chinese churches had started all of the last fourteen churches, with only secondary support from missionaries. The Hong Kong Chinese churches were leading the way in church planting. Likewise, CBTC was now in the hands of a strong localized board with 88 percent of the $142,000 annual budget coming from Hong Kong Christians. The CBTC Board had boldly voted to buy the Huang property in Shatin. With the Lord's help, CBTC would begin the 1998 school year on the new campus.

Third, ABWE's administration approved an Emergency Health Furlough for Lyn and me. With Lyn's health failing, it was not possible for us to continue. I hated to leave Hong Kong at such an exciting and important time, but this was the clear will of the Lord, and we bowed before His wisdom.

The Hong Kong mission field was nearing transition. The Lord had graciously allowed us to see our projects come to fruition, but now it was time for the people of Hong Kong to take over the work.

We were overwhelmed by the farewells. At the CBTC Graduation on May 26, I was named president *emeritus* of the College. On Sunday, June 2, our last Sunday after thirty-one years in Hong Kong, we were invited to Wo Lok Baptist Church for a farewell. Our brothers and sisters in Christ were heartbroken about Lyn and wanted to demonstrate their love for her. At the end of the service, they called us to the front of the church to receive a farewell gift from the four churches that the Lord had allowed us to bring to life. When Pastor Teddy presented us with a check for a brand-new Ford Escort station wagon, we were unable to speak.

On our last day in Hong Kong, the CBTC alumni held a lunch for us, to which most of the graduates came. With all the students, they accompanied us to the airport. Our departure seemed utterly different from our arrival in 1965, when our freighter, the *Pioneer Moor*, slipped into the dock at North Point almost unnoticed. Now, we stood at the airport, surrounded by a crowd of believers and friends, weeping as we embraced for the last time. Leaving was bittersweet, knowing my wife was dying, but also knowing that we had passed the torch to capable local leaders.

One year later, in 1997, Governor Chris Patten would leave the colony, and the Lion Empire would finally relinquish its grasp on the once-barren rock. The Hong Kong believers could not be sure what 1997 would bring when the Dragon Empire claimed back its own. But we were confident that the pastors and churches were prepared to face any eventuality. Lyn and I would be grateful for the rest of our lives that we had had the privilege of living and working in Hong Kong, under the shadow of the dragon.

CHAPTER 25

A MATTER OF OBEDIENCE

When it became clear Lyn could no longer care for herself, and that we would have to leave Hong Kong, it was not difficult for me to know what I needed to do. It was a simple matter of obedience, and I didn't even have to pray about it. Husbands who know Christ are commanded to love their wives "as Christ loved the church" (Ephesians 5:25).

Reading material from the Alzheimer's Association, I was startled by these statistics: if a man was diagnosed with this terrible disease, it was likely his wife would continue to care for him. But if a woman had Alzheimer's, as many as 90 percent of men would abandon her—either physically or emotionally. Some men would literally walk away. Others would leave their wives in a nursing home and not even return to visit.

But if a Christian husband abandons his wife, he blasphemously says, in effect, that Christ only loves the church until trouble arises, then He will turn and run. I saw it as my assignment to learn to love Lyn more and more, "just as, to the degree that" Christ loved the church. For me, that meant to keep Lyn at home and care for her as long as possible. I do not imply it is wrong for a Christian man to put his wife in a nursing home.

Every situation is different, and some have more support from family and church than others. Whatever the circumstances, the husband must always show love and emotional support.

On August 23, 1958, I had promised to love Lyn "in sickness and in health, till death do us part." Now I was determined to keep that promise before God. Kristi and I wanted to keep Lyn at home until the end of her life, if it were possible. We simply asked God to help us to keep Lyn happy and content.

We had not had time to think about what the mission or our supporting churches would say or do. But God had smoothed the way in that area, too. ABWE granted us a one-year Emergency Health Furlough. They extended this several times for an unprecedented total of three and one-half years. Our supporting churches, three-fourths of them in northern Ohio, had supported us since the 1960s. Every one of our churches faithfully continued their support.

We decided to live in Louisiana, where Lyn could be near family. Kristi's husband, Walter Hackney, was pastoring the First Presbyterian Church in Thibodaux, Louisiana, fifty miles southwest of New Orleans. Kristi rented a pleasant apartment for us two miles from the parsonage where they lived. The two-level apartment was triple the size of our last "flat" in Hong Kong. It seemed to be an ideal place for Lyn—finally, she would enjoy the spaciousness she had always craved.

Glenn Schumaker, a good friend of thirty-five years from our home church in Ashland, Ohio, told us he prayed the same prayer every morning: "Lord, please continue to give Lyn clarity as long as You give her life." I didn't know of any Alzheimer's patient who had ever kept clarity till the end of his life, but if the Lord had led Glenn to pray that way, I felt that I should not try to argue with him.

When our children were little, Lyn and I had thrilled at each new learning experience: "I'm a big boy now, Dad. I can take a bath by myself!" We were excited by each new word the children learned. Now we were seeing the process in reverse with Lyn. Each forgotten word produced new trauma. By coincidence, our grandson, Walter Gordon, was learning to tie his shoelaces at the same time Lyn was forgetting how to tie hers.

I entered a new school, the school of learning things I had never had to do before. I found a cookbook and tried to cook food Lyn would not just endure, but also enjoy. I washed the clothes and learned to iron fairly well. Sometimes I struggled: Was it kindness or cruelty to let Lyn take thirty minutes to wash a few dishes that I could do in three minutes? I soon realized that in seminary there had been no courses in how to wash and set a woman's hair.

I tried to keep Lyn walking, but her body seemed to be weakening along with her once-brilliant mind. Since she could no longer read, I read to her for long periods. We read the Bible, history books, and biographies. Our daughter, Lori, recommended Jan Karon's fictional Mitford series about Father Tim, an Episcopalian rector. Lyn seemed to enjoy those books. Snuggled beside me on the couch, with my arm around her, she seemed content. For three years, she never stopped smiling and trying to thank us for making her comfortable.

By the spring of 1997, she had more trouble speaking, and sometimes even after playing "Twenty Questions," we still could not understand her. She could only walk now with great difficulty, and she was no longer able to feed herself well. The first time I had to put a spoon to her mouth, feeding her like a baby, Kristi had to turn away so we would not see her tears.

We began to battle the problem of Lyn's depression and repeatedly had to answer Lyn's question, "What is happening to me? I feel like a baby." We always tried to explain patiently about her disease. But we never failed to reassure her, "Kristi and I are going to keep you at home and care for you. We will *never* leave you. The last thing you will see on this earth will be my face, smiling at you with all my love—and the first thing you will see in the next world will be the face of Jesus, which will be far better!" That usually seemed to comfort her.

The doctor prescribed one medicine that helped her depression, and a new Alzheimer's drug, Aricept, seemed to preserve her clarity for more than a year. Lyn loved to watch a mother bird bring bugs and seeds to feed her three babies nestled in a tree outside our living room window. I was able to remind her, "Your heavenly Father feeds them. Are you not of more value than they?" (Matthew 6:26).

By Christmas of 1997, we began to use a wheelchair and a handicapped parking permit. Pastor Teddy and Jennifer came to Louisiana to visit, and Dr. Edwin Fung also visited. He claimed, "I was close by," though he had really been in San Francisco for a medical convention.

By the spring of 1998, Kristi and I realized Lyn would not be able to climb the stairs much longer, and as she continued to fail, I might be unable to care for her alone, twenty-four hours a day. We began to pray about side-by-side housing. Then Kristi asked Walter if he would pray about getting more involved in Lyn's care. Walter answered, "No, I won't pray about it. Unless someone has taken the fifth commandment, 'Honor thy father and thy mother,' out of the Bible, I won't pray about it, I will *do* it."

In a selfless act of love and devotion, Walter resigned his pastorate of six years and accepted a job teaching high school math in Rockford, Illinois. By August 10, Walter and Kristi had driven to Rockford and purchased a home that would ideally suit Lyn. Walter's own mother had died of cancer when he was only eight. Since he had been unable to help her, he told me he would consider it a privilege to help Lyn.

Everything about the house in Rockford was ideal. It was a duplex on a peaceful street, one block away from a picturesque bike path. We lived on one side, Kristi lived on the other. It was on one level, so Lyn was saved from climbing stairs, and the indoor access to Kristi's side was perfect for Rockford's cold winters.

The front and back yards were bursting with roses, birds, and the green grass Lyn had missed so much during her thirty-one years in Hong Kong. We were just two miles from Lyn's sister, Lura, who had always been close to Lyn. As a nurse, Lura was able to help care for Lyn. She was ready to answer my questions day or night.

When we moved in October 1998, Lyn seemed to have reached a plateau. She was still walking, though it was really more of a shuffle. She was still talking, though not usually in complete sentences. She still laughed and smiled. The neighborhood was filled with hundreds of tall trees with their colors turning. Her favorite words were "Pretty" and "Wow!" Every day I pushed her for two or three miles in the wheelchair. One unusually tall weeping willow often caught her attention. "Look at your favorite tree, Lyn," I would say. "Do you remember what Jesus said? 'Not even Solomon in all his glory was arrayed like one of these'" (Matthew 6:29). That almost always caused her to smile.

We attended New Life Baptist Church in Lake-in-the-Hills, Illinois. This was a church started by Mark and Judy Wood, who had been coworkers in Hong Kong in the late 1980s. It was a forty-mile drive, but we wanted to help, if even only a very little, in a church-planting effort. More importantly, the people always greeted Lyn so warmly that she would break into a big smile. She made it obvious that she looked forward to returning. But we were only able to attend New Life for eight months. In May 1999, a family conference agreed that due to Lyn's increasing incontinence, and her decreasing comprehension and walking ability, it was now more of a burden than a blessing for her to attend church. I took her for the last time on Mother's Day.

One day in September, as I walked beneath the beautiful trees, I repeated a prayer I had often prayed during those months, "Lord, if it would please You, please take Lyn home to heaven before she suffers the terrible dehumanization that so often accompanies this disease." I always closed my prayer by adding,

"Nevertheless, not my will, Father, but Yours, be done." Later I discovered that *many* of our friends had been praying that way. Three days later Lyn contracted a urinary tract infection, a virulent viral flu that did not respond to antibiotics, and had a stroke, all at the same time. Lyn's brother, John, tried to comfort me with the words of C. S. Lewis: "Harry, this is a 'severe mercy.'"

She lost all ability to walk, stand, or sit. She could not control her bladder, say more than just a word or two, nor swallow food or even liquids. She ran a fever for most of the next three weeks. She slept much of the time, and when she was awake, she sat with her head drooping to one side. A therapist came to the house and said that there was damage to the left hemisphere of her brain.

On October 1, the visiting nurse, in consultation with our Christian doctor and friend, William Edgren, urged us to take Lyn to the hospital. She was extremely dehydrated, as she had been taking little fluid and almost no food. Lyn would have to be transported by ambulance since she could not even sit up. The emergency room doctor, also a Christian, was the first one to tell us that Lyn had perhaps two weeks to live. Over the weekend, several nurses and Dr. Edgren agreed. The doctors commended us for our care—Lyn did not have a single bedsore. Kris was relieved at the praise; she had worked tenaciously to protect Lyn's fragile skin.

Lyn returned home on October 4, and we brought visiting nurses in to help. She lost weight and began to look gaunt. But she still smiled, recognized us, and said a word or two. On October 16, she asked her last question: "If we die?" I tried to describe again the glories of heaven and reminded Lyn that she would soon see Jesus, and her brother, Jimmy, who had died when he was only nineteen, over forty years before. She responded with just one word: "Goody!"

On October 23, she told me, "I love you," for the last time, and lapsed into a semiconscious condition. The doctors and nurses told us she was in the last forty-eight hours. In one of the finest gestures of love that I had ever seen, Teddy arrived all the way from Hong Kong to visit Lyn. She was able to smile at him, and whispered, "Hello," which was a thrill to him.

On Wednesday, October 27, 1999, our ABWE administrator and close friend for thirty years, Bill Commons, came from Ohio to see Lyn, and Mark and Judy Wood drove up the same afternoon. They all stood around the bed with Kristi and sang some of Lyn's favorite songs. She opened her eyes and smiled at them. Glenn Schumaker's prayer had been answered—Lyn had kept a measure of clarity to the end of her life. She died several hours later, at 4:22 p.m., with family surrounding her bed.

We knew that our home church would not be large enough to hold the crowd, so the memorial service was held at one of our supporting churches, Northfield Baptist Church in Ohio, on November 6. Brent and Clare flew in from Hong Kong, and Lori from Boston. Among the 300 who gathered at the memorial service were eight believers from Hong Kong. Teddy had flown back again for the service—crossing the Pacific four times in just a few weeks—bringing Jennifer with him. Dr. and Mrs. Daniel Chung, who had served at Sunshine and Evangel Baptist in the 1960s were there, along with Edmund Kwan from our days at Calvary Baptist, and Wong Yee-shing from the early days in Kwun Tong. Dr. Edwin Fung had been in Lyn's Sunday school class in Wo Lok and had tried so hard to help after Lyn's illness. Longtime friend Yeung Po-wan came from Toronto, Canada, where he and Miranda had started two thriving churches. All these men had experienced the impact of Lyn's love. It was an incredible testimony to Lyn's influence on the lives of Hong Kong believers.

At the memorial service, Brent told a story that seemed to epitomize Lyn. When he was eight, we were on furlough in Ohio. Brent was frustrated because he didn't fit in well with the other American boys. For his birthday, we gave him a sleeping bag with the names and logos of all the NFL pro football teams on it, so he could feel like a "real" American. He kept it for years, as one of his favorite possessions. Years later, as a college student, Brent returned to Hong Kong, staying with us at the Ferry Street apartment.

When a winter cold snap set in, he knew Lyn would be worrying about the poor, homeless street-sleepers. One bitter night he walked the half-mile from our apartment to the Bible college. Knowing his mother was particularly concerned about one man, Brent searched for him under the flyover. There he was, huddled under Brent's NFL sleeping bag! Until that minute, he had never known that Lyn had given it away. That acting out of her love was what Brent remembered most about his Mom. It was what we all remember. We are so much the richer for having known her.

Nahum 1:7 and Psalm 100:5 both say, "The Lord is good." For thirty-six years of our forty-one-year marriage, I ministered with Lyn. For the last three and one-half years, I ministered to Lyn—every hour, every day. He enabled me to honor my vows. The Lord has indeed been good.

EPILOGUE

During the years I was caring for Lyn, I thought that if the Lord ever freed me for ministry again, I would return to Hong Kong as soon as possible. But as months of care giving stretched into three years, the situation in Hong Kong changed. At CBTC, we always set criteria to be met before a student is ready to graduate. It was always a happy moment when the dean turned to me during the ceremony and said, "Mr. President, this student has met the requirements and is ready to graduate!" Now, it became clear to me that Hong Kong was a mission field in transition and, like its students, had met the criteria for graduation to the next level, in which national believers take the leadership roles.

First, the Hong Kong team had effectively tackled *evangelism*. When we took the survey in 1985, the missionaries and the Chinese pastors had agreed to aim for two goals: making the Bible college independent and growing from fifteen to twenty-five independent churches by 1996. By 1996, these goals had not only been reached—they had been surpassed. CBTC had become an independent college and ABWE had thirty-three churches, all independent or being steered by other Chinese churches. The college had supplied twenty-six leaders for these churches.

Today, a new generation of bold, innovative Chinese church planters has emerged in Hong Kong. Calvary Baptist Church has grown into an outstanding church-planting congregation. P. K. Wong, who had been a small boy in the junior church at Calvary which Jean Shawver and Lyn started in 1968, attended CBTC. After graduating in 1987, P.K. pastored Grace Baptist, one of Calvary's daughter churches. When the dynamic Steve Trinh left Hong Kong to go to Australia as a missionary church planter in 1992, Calvary called P.K. to be its senior pastor. Though it could have grown to be a very large church, Calvary made a deliberate choice to send its best members to start new churches all over the city. Now, Calvary averages only 200, but 700 more meet in nine daughter and granddaughter churches.

Evangel Baptist Church has followed the same pattern. It averaged 340 people in 1989, but today, under the leadership of Calvin Lam and Moses Law, Evangel has close to 200 people in the mother church and 300 others in three daughter churches. Heritage Baptist Church, where Timothy Ng (CBTC 1990) has served for ten years, averaged over 300 for ten years and helped start two daughter churches.

In our last five or six years in Hong Kong, as president of CBTC, I was regularly invited to represent the college. Over a period of time, I had the privilege of speaking in Cantonese in almost all of ABWE's churches. Week after week, I visited enthusiastic congregations that were growing and reaching out to their neighborhoods. Most of the churches were filled with young people. It was clear to me that evangelism remains a top priority of these Hong Kong churches.

A second criterion that shows a mission field ready to move to the next level of maturity is the development of *leadership*. In addition to the excellent team at CBTC, God raised up outstanding leaders in Hong Kong. Barnabas Chung (CBTC 1990) recently left a fine pastorate at Tin Yue Baptist Church in the New Territories to become the executive secretary of the ABWE

Fellowship of Churches. The pastors leading our churches today are young, but capable, men. The principle of internship, around which we rebuilt CBTC, has been the key to developing leadership. The "students" have not only become "like their teachers," they have far surpassed us.

As Hong Kong changes, the new generation of Chinese leaders has shown great wisdom in adapting their methods to the times. ABWE missionaries used clinics in the 1960s and 1970s and then found study centers and kindergartens to be effective tools for starting churches in the 1980s and 1990s. But since the handover to China in 1997, the economy has fallen drastically, and the new government has continually increased rents on these centers. At the same time, the numbers of young children and teenagers in Hong Kong has been dropping, causing decreasing enrollments. Now some of our churches have decided to return these centers to the government. They were never an end, merely a means of church planting. Heritage is closing its kindergarten in 2003, and Wo Lok will give back its study center in 2004. Both of the churches will then move to purchased premises.

A third criterion is *cheerful giving*. Many of the Christians in Hong Kong today not only have good jobs and are prospering, they are also willing to give generously to the Lord's work. The story of the Chungs is but one example of the incredible giving I have seen over and over again from Chinese believers.

In the early 1990s, CBTC graduates Jeremiah and Loretta Chung told us that the Lord was leading them to go as missionaries to Vanuatu (known as the New Hebrides until its independence in 1980), a small group of islands in the South Pacific just east of the Coral Sea. While they were studying linguistics in Singapore, Jeremiah asked me how long I thought it would take for them to raise their support. I knew that missionary appointees in the United States were taking two years or more to get to the field. I predicted the Chungs might need six months and promised we would pray that the Lord would provide for them in that time. My prediction was wide of the mark. In a single *afternoon,* a group of pastors, with the authorization of their churches, met and promised *all* of the Chungs' needed support. I was never happier to be proven wrong.

ABWE has long desired to start not only church plants, but church-planting movements that would result in missions movements. In Hong Kong we have seen a textbook church-planting movement—an almost exponential increase of indigenous churches planting churches. Calvary has become nine churches, Evangel four, and now these churches are sending out missionaries to other parts of the world. The Chungs are among the first members of a Hong Kong missions movement.

As this movement continues to develop, ABWE is now recruiting missionaries to work in a partnership role with the Hong Kong churches, setting new goals for church planting and continued improvement of the Bible college. If missionaries were to try to take the lead in church planting again, it would be like taking a step backward. The churches are fully independent, growing under Chinese pastors, and the China Baptist Theological College continues to flourish under the leadership of Dr. Teddy Cheng. In January 2003, CBTC broke ground for a new campus on the Huang property on a hill in the New Territories overlooking the satellite city of Shatin. Meanwhile, Dave and Peggy Pardini, Sue Farley, and Chris and Maylin Hartwick form an excellent transition team that I believe God has clearly raised up "for such a time as this."

In Hong Kong, the new government allows its people freedoms similar to those under the previous British administration. The worst fears of tanks in the streets or newspapers being pressed into the service of propaganda have not yet been realized. But in July 2003, 500,000 people marched in the streets of Hong Kong to protest against Article 23, the government's proposed anti-sedition law. If passed, the law could bring major restrictions in the freedoms promised to Hong Kong's people until at least

2047, according to the Joint Declaration signed by China and Great Britain. Now that Hong Kong has ceased to be in the mere shadow of the dragon and has been absorbed back into the Dragon Empire itself, an uneasy truce continues between "one country" and "two systems."

I cannot predict what the twenty-first century will hold for Hong Kong, whether political turmoil or long-craved democracy, but I remain certain that even if believers encounter the persecution Christians have faced on the mainland, God will continue to bless the growing church in Hong Kong.

* * *

Around the time I realized that my returning to Hong Kong would be a step in the wrong direction, I began to receive dozens of invitations to teach training modules in many other countries, particularly in Asia. Thousands of pastors and church leaders around the world serve the Lord with great zeal, but lack all except a very simple level of training. God gave me a burden to train and equip these pastors for better leadership.

In April 2000, I accepted the ABWE Board's new assignment as "International Professor of Theological Education and Missiology." I had already taught modules in Asia Baptist Theological Seminary's six teaching sites—Hong Kong, Singapore, Manila, Iloilo, Bangkok, and Rangoon—since the school opened in 1983. In the past three years, I have taught four modules for ABTS each year and other courses in twenty-three countries on all six continents. Today, when not traveling or teaching, I continue to live in the duplex in Rockford, Illinois, next door to Kristi and Walter, and grandchildren Anne and Walter Gordon. Lori lives in Salem, Massachusetts, and teaches English and Creative Writing at Gordon College and at Salem State University. Brent and Clare work in London, where they moved in 2001 after spending their whole lives in Hong Kong.

In my new ministry, I often see the missionary stories that I loved as a student and taught in my missions classes at CBTC come alive in startling new ways. One story which always fascinated me took place in the New Hebrides islands in the South Pacific. In 1839, islanders clubbed missionary John Williams to death, cooked him, and ate his body. When Scotsman John Paton announced his intention to take William's place, one Mr. Dickson objected: "The cannibals! You will be eaten by cannibals!"

Paton responded: "Mr. Dickson, you are advanced in years now, and your own prospect is soon to be laid in the grave, there to be eaten by worms. I confess to you, that if I can but live and die serving and honoring the Lord Jesus, it will make no difference to me whether I am eaten by cannibals or by worms. And in the Great Day my resurrection body will rise as fair as yours in the likeness of our risen redeemer."

Paton arrived in the New Hebrides in 1858. Less than a year later, he buried his wife and new baby son there. Over the years, despite Paton's heroic efforts, response to the Gospel was extremely slow.

In November 2000, I visited Jeremiah and Loretta Chung, the Hong Kong couple whose support had been raised so quickly, in their new home in the former New Hebrides, now renamed the Republic of Vanuatu. They live in the village of Navale, the most primitive place I have ever seen in the fifty-one countries I have visited. From the town of Luganville, we rode two hours in a four-wheel-drive truck, fording six rivers. Then we hiked for thirty minutes, crossing two more rivers. There was no electricity or running water in this town near the equator, so we washed each night in the river.

One afternoon, Norman, a tall, six-foot national, asked to speak with me. He has been helping the Chungs translate the Scriptures into the Merei language, one slow chapter at a time. Three afternoons each week, Norman, the descendant of the cannibals who killed John Williams, takes ten newly translated verses from Matthew's Gospel, walks over the hills, and teaches them in the next village. He asked me, "Was there some verse in the Bible that told you to care for your wife during her last illness?"

Though he had translated Mark, Acts, and I and II Timothy into Merei with the Chungs, and he was just starting Matthew, Norman had not yet reached Ephesians. We sat in a hut together, and I outlined Ephesians for him, particularly Ephesians 5:25, that verse which has become so meaningful to me: "Husbands, love your wives, just as Christ also loved the church."

As we conversed, I marveled at how John Williams' death and John Paton's sacrifice, like Robert Morrison's in China, were finally being redeemed by God over a century later, as nationals like Norman responded to the Gospel. I thank God for my assignment to build into the lives of Norman and the Chungs and other valiant believers in every corner of the world— whether in the urban jungles of Hong Kong or the primitive villages of the Pacific islands.

NOTES

PROLOGUE
1. *Hong Kong Standard,* February 15, 1988.

CHAPTER 1
1. A. J. Broomhall, *Hudson Taylor and China's Open Century,* Volume 1 (London: Hodder & Stoughton, 1981), p. 119.
2. Austin Coates, *A Macao Narrative* (Heinemann: Hong Kong, 1978), p. 21.
3. Ibid., p. 58.
4. Jonathan D. Spence, *The Search for Modern China* (New York: W. W. Norton and Company, 1990), p. 129.
5. A. J. Broomhall, op. cit., Volume 1, p. 199.
6. Perhaps the best biography of Morrison is that of Marshall Broomhall, *Robert Morrison: A Master-builder* (New York: Doran, 1924). For a shorter treatment, see Ruth A. Tucker, *From Jerusalem to Irian Jaya* (Grand Rapids, Michigan: Zondervan, 1983), pp. 166–171.
7. A. J. Broomhall, op. cit., p. 219.
8. A. J. Broomhall, op. cit., p. 213.
9. It is hard to find conclusive proof either way. Note that different books use different systems of spelling Chinese names.
10. A. J. Broomhall, op. cit., p. 245.
11. Austin Coates, op. cit., p. 82.
12. Ibid., p. 82.
13. Jonathan D. Spence, op. cit., p. 156.
14. A. J. Broomhall, op. cit., Volume III, p. 214.
15. Ruth Tucker, op. cit., p. 173.
16. Ibid., p. 182.

CHAPTER 2

1. *Hong Kong 1967* (Hong Kong: Government Press, 1968), p. 256–257. Unless otherwise noted, all population and geographical statistics cited in this book are from the Hong Kong Government Press yearbooks, 1963-2000.
2. Ibid., p. 259.
3. Jonathan Dimbleby, *The Last Governor* (London: Warner Books, 1997), p. 118.
4. *Hong Kong 1996* (Hong Kong: Government Press, 1997), p. 407.
5. Jonathan Spence, op. cit., p. 231.
6. *Hong Kong 1960* (Hong Kong: Government Press, 1961), p. 37.
7. *Hong Kong 1964* (Hong Kong: Government Press, 1965), p. 266.
8. A. J. Broomhall, op. cit., Volume VII, p. 566, 1965.
9. Philip Short, *Mao: A Life* (New York: Henry Holt and Company, 1999), p. 419.
10. A. J. Broomhall, op. cit., Volume VII (London: Hodder and Stoughton, 1989), p. 563.
11. Ibid., p. 564.
12. Ibid., p. 567.
13. Gerald Anderson, Ed., *Biographical Dictionary of Christian Missions* (New York: Macmillan Reference USA, 1998), p. 716.
14. For descriptions of Hong Kong, I am indebted to *Hong Kong in Focus* (Philadelphia: Association of Baptists for World Evangelism, 1968), large sections of which were written by my wife, Lyn.
15. *Hong Kong 1963* (Hong Kong Government Press, 1964), p. 35.

CHAPTER 3

1. See Marjorie Barnett Miller, *Pearl from the Orient* (Harrisburg: ABWE Publishing, 2001).
2. *Hong Kong 1963,* op. cit., p. 368.
3. Robert Cottrell, *The End of Hong Kong* (London: John Murray, 1993), p. 27.

CHAPTER 4

1. Robert Cottrell, op. cit., p. 28.
2. *Hong Kong 1965* (Hong Kong: Government Press, 1966), p. 235.

CHAPTER 5

1. *Hong Kong 1987* (Hong Kong: Government Press, 1988), p. 249.

CHAPTER 6

1. See Chik Hon Man and Ng Lam Sun Yuk, *Chinese-English Dictionary* (Hong Kong: New Asia Yale in China Language Center, 1989).
2. Dr. and Mrs. Howard Taylor, *Hudson Taylor in Early Years* (London: China Inland Mission, 1911), p. 86.

CHAPTER 7

1. *Hong Kong 1967* (Hong Kong Government Press, 1968), pp. 127, 329.
2. Dr. Anderson, "The Professor Goes to the Far East," *The Standard* (November 1, 1977), p. 16.

CHAPTER 8

1. Philip Short, op. cit., p. 505.
2. Jonathan Spence, op. cit., p. 606.
3. Philip Short, op. cit., p. 563.
4. Jonathan Spence, op cit., p. 611.
5. *Hong Kong 1967,* op. cit., p. 3.
6. *Hong Kong 1963,* op. cit., p. 240.
7. *Hong Kong 1967,* op. cit., p. 166.
8. Ibid., p. 166.

CHAPTER 9

1. *Hong Kong 1967,* op. cit., p. 52. Hong Kong's population as a whole had passed four million.
2. The mission has since changed this policy, and we would be allowed to buy an apartment like that today.

CHAPTER 11

1. Jonathan Spence, op. cit., p. 633.

CHAPTER 12

1. Norris and Ross McWhirter, Editors, *Guinness Book of Records* (Middlesex, England: Guinness Superlatives Limited, 1971).
2. *South China Morning Post,* January 5, 1976.
3. C. P. Lo, *Hong Kong* (London: Belhaven Press, 1992), p. 126.
4. A. B. Bruce, *The Training of the Twelve* (Grand Rapids: Kregel Publications, 1971), p. 30.

CHAPTER 13

1. Norman Johnson and John W. Peterson, Compilers, *Folk Hymnal* (Grand Rapids, Michigan: Singspiration Music, 1970), p. 74.

CHAPTER 14

1. Jonathan Spence, op. cit., p. 654.

CHAPTER 15

1. Jonathan Spence, op. cit., p. 649.
2. Howard and Phyllis Rutledge, *In the Presence of Mine Enemies* (Old Tappan, New Jersey: Fleming H. Revell Company, 1973).
3. Tim LaHaye, *How to Study the Bible for Yourself* (Irvine, California: Harvest House Publishers, 1976).

CHAPTER 16

1. *Message* (Cherry Hill, New Jersey: Association of Baptists for World Evangelism, September–October, 1979), p. 16.

CHAPTER 17

1. Mark Roberti, *The Fall of Hong Kong: China's Triumph and Britain's Betrayal* (New York: John Wiley and Sons, 1994), p. 22–23.
2. Ibid., pp. 24–25.
3. Ibid., p. 25.
4. *Hong Kong 1980* (Hong Kong: Government Press, 1981), p. 259.

CHAPTER 18

1. *Hong Kong 1980,* op. cit., p. 206.

CHAPTER 19

1. Robert Cottrell, op. cit., p. 150.
2. See Harry Ambacher, "Hong Kong—Out of Space, Out of Time" (*Baptist Bulletin*, June 1985), pp. 11–13.
3. Jonathan Spence, op. cit., pp. 710–711.
4. *Time,* September 17, 1984.
5. Mark Roberti, op. cit., p. 304.

CHAPTER 20

1. Mark Roberti, op. cit., p. 26.

CHAPTER 21

1. David Goodman, *Beijing Street Voices: The Poetry and Politics of China's Democracy Movement* (London: 1981), p. 79.
2. The capital city was called Peking until October 1949, when the new Communist government renamed it Beijing.
3. Jonathan Spence, op. cit., p. 311.
4. *International Herald Tribune,* February 7, 1987.
5. *South China Morning Post,* October 15, 1987.
6. *Hong Kong Standard,* September 19, 1987.
7. *International Herald Tribune,* June 13, 1988.
8. *Time,* July 11, 1988.
9. Jonathan Spence, op. cit., p. 739.
10. Ibid., p. 741.
11. *South China Morning Post,* May 22, 1989.
12. David Morrison, Ed., *Massacre in Beijing* (New York: Time, Inc. Books, 1989), p. 35.
13. Jonathan Spence, op. cit., p. 743.
14. Ibid.
15. David Morrison, op. cit., p. 53.
16. *Hong Kong 1990* (Hong Kong Government Press, 1991), p. 2.
17. See Melinda Liu, *Beijing Spring* (Hong Kong: Asia 2000, 1989) and Yi Mu and Mark V. Thompson, *Crisis at Tiananmen* (San Francisco: China Books, 1989).

CHAPTER 23

1. *Hong Kong 1996* (Hong Kong: Government Press, 1997), p. 5
2. Chris Patten, *East and West* (London: Macmillan, 1998), p. 69.
3. *Hong Kong 1990,* op. cit., p. 200.

SELECTED BIBLIOGRAPHY

Broomhall, A. J. *Hudson Taylor and China's Open Century,* Volumes I–VII. London: Hodder and Stoughton, 1981–1989.

Broomhall, Marshall. *Robert Morrison: A Master Builder.* New York: Doran, 1924.

Coates, Austin. *A Macao Narrative.* Hong Kong: Heinemann, 1978.

Cottrell, Robert. *The End of Hong Kong.* London: John Murray, 1993.

Dimbleby, Jonathan. *The Last Governor.* London: Warner Books, 1997.

Liu, Melinda. *Beijing Spring.* Hong Kong: Asia 2000 Ltd., 1989.

Miller, Marjory Barnett. *Pearl from the Orient.* Harrisburg, PA: ABWE Publishing, 2001.

Morrison, Donald, Ed. *Massacre in Beijing.* New York: Time, Inc. Books, 1989.

Patten, Chris. *East and West.* London: Macmillan, 1998.

Short, Philip. *Mao: A Life.* New York: Henry Holt and Company, 1999.

Spence, Jonathan D. *The Search for Modern China.* New York: W. W. Norton & Company, 1990.

Thompson, Yi Mu and Mark V. *Crisis at Tiananmen.* San Francisco: China Books, 1989.

Tucker, Ruth A. *From Jerusalem to Irian Jaya.* Grand Rapids, Michigan: Zondervan, 1983.

THE HONG KONG FIELD COUNCIL
1951–2001

Victor and Margaret Barnett 1951–1965
William Reid 1955–1985
Joan Reid 1955–1969
Dortha Warner 1955–1971
Ruth Warner 1955–1980
Jaymes and Dorothy Morgan 1959–1976
Frank and Sophie Jenista 1959–1960
Starling Post 1959–1970
Bessie Turnbull 1962–1964
Gladys MacLean 1962–1964
Richard and Marion Morey 1964–1966
Robert and Margaret Paswaters 1964–1999
Carson and Darline Fremont 1964–1993
Harry and Lyn Ambacher 1965–1996
Jean Shawver 1966–1973
Donald and Ruth Trott 1966–1970
William and Sharon Commons 1967–1980
Robert and Sandra Hedrick 1969–1978
Robert and Pat Henry 1969–1978
Melvin and Julia Lacock 1973–1982
Carol Bibighaus 1974–1994
Violet Hart 1975–1979
Gloria Reid 1975–1985
Susanne Farley 1976–present
Alice Augsburger 1977–1979
Norman and Louise Barnard 1977–1990
David and Peggy Pardini 1982–present
Mark and Judy Wood 1986–1989
Craig and Darlene Kordic 1988–1996
Marvin and Ruth Humphreys 1991–1993
Chris and Maylin Hartwick 1996–present

ABWE HONG KONG CHURCHES

AVERAGE WORSHIP SERVICE ATTENDANCE

Church Name / Year Founded / Founded By	1960	1964	1969	1974	1979	1984	1989	1994	1999
Evangel — 1953 — Barnetts	40	100	88	80	95	150	340	119	170
Calvary — 1956 — Reids	30	60	60	104	226	246	337	211	175
Wo Lok — 1971 — Ambachers				20	26	107	151	129	113
Heritage — 1972 — Paswaterses				130	223	228	267	319	323
Kwai Shing — 1972 — Commonses				50	158	160	152	110	78
Chung On — 1978 — Commonses & Kwai Shing					44	90	90	93	100
Pak Tin — 1980 — Calvary					30	104	165	117	103
Abundant Grace — 1981 — Calvary						88	135	110	90
Tsuen Wan — 1981 — Kwai Shing						40	44	42	40
Cheung Hong — 1982 — Heritage						30	76	110	100
Glorious Word — 1983 — Evangel			43	19	25	45	73	82	90
Shun On — 1983 — Ambachers & Wo Lok						35	91	110	104

Average Attendance by Year

Church Name Year Founded Founded By	Average Attendance by Year								
	1960	1964	1969	1974	1979	1984	1989	1994	1999
Tai Hing 1983 Paswaterses						34	47	88	93
Lai King 1984 Barnards & Chung On (Kwai Hing)							48	56	45
Heng On 1988 Paswaterses & Calvary							116	118	119
Po Lam 1988 Ambachers & Wo Lok							30	44	45
Shek Yam 1989 Evangel							80	118	126
Engraving Grace 1990 Abundant Grace								42	45
Grace 1990 Calvary								100	105
Garden Estate 1991 Ambachers & Wo Lok								60	68
Tin Yue 1991 Pardinis & Kwai Shing								50	56
Grace Seal 1992 Pak Tin								55	48
Un Chau 1992 Chung On									64
Manifesting Grace 1993 Calvary								25	40
Jordan 1993 Evangel								70	72
Exalting Grace 1994 Calvary									59

Church Name Year Founded Founded By	Average Attendance by Year								
	1960	1964	1969	1974	1979	1984	1989	1994	1999
Prosperous Garden 1995 Paswaterses & Heritage									32
Shing Yan 1996 Hartwicks & Kwai Shing									31
Luk Yeung 1997 Paswaterses & Kwai Shing									34
Shine 1997 Calvary									76
Lei Muk Shue 1999 Chung On									
Shun On—Tai Kok Tsui 2000 Shun On									

BIOGRAPHY

Harry and Lyn Ambacher joined ABWE in 1962, fully antic-
ipating a career of missionary service in Bangladesh. But God
intervened and sent them to Hong Kong in 1965, where they
served faithfully for thirty-one years. *Under the Shadow of the
Dragon* traces the development of the ABWE church-planting
ministry in Hong Kong through a phenomenal time of growth.
The Ambachers worked together with nationals to plant four
churches, which today are all independent. Harry also helped to
start the China Baptist Theological College in 1966 and served
as its president for twenty-one years.

In 1994, Lyn was diagnosed with early onset Alzheimer's disease. They were able to go back to Hong Kong for a time, but
most of the next several years were devoted to caring for Lyn's
deteriorating condition. Lyn went to be with the Lord on
October 27, 1999. Harry has become ABWE's international professor of theological education and missiology. He has taught
modules in the Asia Baptist Theological Seminary and in twenty-
three other countries around the world.

If you enjoyed the Ambacher story
from Hong Kong, you'll want to
read about the Barnetts—
ABWE's early missionaries
to Hong Kong and China.

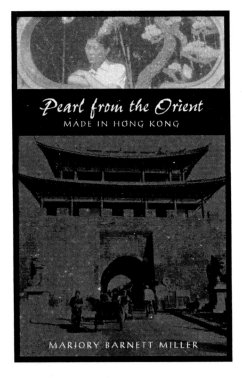

Pearl from the Orient
by Marjory Barnett Miller

Marjory was born in Hong
Kong to Victor and Margaret
Barnett, ABWE's first missionaries to China. She lived all
of her childhood in China,
speaking two Chinese dialects
fluently before she learned
English. Among the many
incredible experiences Marjory
relates in *Pearl from the Orient*
are harrowing escapes from
Japanese invaders and Communist insurgents, surviving the
war on one meal a day, helping
her parents dispense medical
care during epidemics, and
many other amazing events.
Pearl from the Orient clearly
shows how God protects and
provides for his servants.

Suggested Donation: $12.00
(includes shipping and handling)

*Find other great books from
ABWE Publishing online at
www.abwe.org*

How to Order

Write to: ABWE Publishing
P.O. Box 8585
Harrisburg, PA 17105

Call toll-free: 1-877-959-2293

E-mail: publish@abwe.org